PENGUIN
THE ESSENTIAL DE

Priti Narain belongs to an old family of Delhi and a community which
has a tradition of taking great pains over the preparation and serving of
good food. She ran a gourmet restaurant in Delhi for two years, in
partnership with a friend. For several years, she also supplied cakes on
order.

Currently Priti leads a relaxed life, bird-watching and taking the
occasional order for chocolate cake.

THE
ESSENTIAL DELHI
COOKBOOK

Priti Narain

PENGUIN BOOKS

PENGUIN BOOKS

Published by the Penguin Group

Penguin Books India Pvt. Ltd, 7th Floor, Infinity Tower C, DLF Cyber City,
Gurgaon 122 002, Haryana, India

Penguin Group (USA) Inc., 375 Hudson Street, New York, New York 10014, USA

Penguin Group (Canada), 90 Eglinton Avenue East, Suite 700, Toronto, Ontario,
M4P 2Y3, Canada

Penguin Books Ltd, 80 Strand, London WC2R 0RL, England

Penguin Ireland, 25 St Stephen's Green, Dublin 2, Ireland (a division of Penguin
Books Ltd)

Penguin Group (Australia), 707 Collins Street, Melbourne, Victoria 3008, Australia

Penguin Group (NZ), 67 Apollo Drive, Rosedale, Auckland 0632, New Zealand

Penguin Books (South Africa) (Pty) Ltd, Block D, Rosebank Office Park, 181 Jan
Smuts Avenue, Parktown North, Johannesburg 2193, South Africa

Penguin Books Ltd, Registered Offices: 80 Strand, London WC2R 0RL, England

First published by Penguin Books India 2000

Copyright © Priti Narain 2000

Series Editor: Bhikoo J. Manekshaw

Illustrations by Amitabh

All rights reserved

12 11 10 9 8 7 6

ISBN 9780140293265

Typeset in Garamond by Digital Technologies and Printing Solutions, New Delhi
Printed at Repro India Ltd, Navi Mumbai

A PENGUIN RANDOM HOUSE COMPANY

To
Brijesh with love

An Aborigine of Delhi

An Australian gentleman once asked
my father to which part of the
country he belonged. On hearing the
reply 'Delhi', he expressed surprise
and said, 'Surely you mean U.P.?
How can anyone belong to Delhi?'
My father replied that his ancestors
had worked in the Mughal courts and
that several generations of his family
had lived in Delhi. The Australian
gentleman called to his wife and said,
'Dear, come and meet an aborigine of
Delhi.'
This is a book from one of the
'aborigines of Delhi'.

Contents

Acknowledgements

This book would not have been written had it not been for Mrs Bhicoo Manekshaw. As part of her crusade for preserving traditional recipes from each region of India she practically bullied me into undertaking this task. I am indeed grateful to her as Delhi Food has been an exciting voyage of discovery.

I have received support and encouragement from a myriad of my friends and family. Many have shared their recipes, experiences and memories. I am particularly indebted to Zakia Zaheer, Mrs Maheshwar Dayal, Manju Vira, Babu Shahi as well as Kusum Khanna, Teeny Pershad, Aruna Kumar and Usha Malik. I must also thank my sisters-in-law Nina Shanker, Urmila Mathur and Sushma Seth.

My sister Malti Nehru and my brother-in-law Jaiwant Paul helped with the text; my daughter-in-law Ketaki patiently read through every recipe and discovered missing ingredients—any omissions that remain are entirely mine. I also thank my son Varun who made me computer literate and handled all the jobs that were beyond me; and most of all my husband Brijesh who has always believed that every new recipe I tried would be successful. I am also grateful to Sherna Wadia who has painstakingly edited the work and made many helpful suggestions and V.K. Karthika of Penguin India who has been very understanding about deadlines as the project has taken longer than I had anticipated.

Introduction

Delhi has had a chequered history and there have been many different influences on the cuisine and culture of the people.

The Kauravs and Pandavas, who lived around what we now call Delhi, seem to have had a rich cuisine. The Mahabharat mentions dishes made of milk and rice mixed with ghee, honey and roots. Rice was also cooked with meat. There are descriptions of meat roasted on spits, curries of meat and fruit seasoned with fragrant spices. The meats eaten include those of pig, deer, cow, sheep, birds and even donkey and camel!

After the excesses of the Mahabharat era, the food habits became simpler and seem to have become quite austere. Vegetarianism developed among the Brahmins, and under the influence of Buddhism and Jainism the common people followed suit. Onions and garlic stopped being widely used as they were considered foods which aroused man's baser instincts, e.g. lust, anger etc. They were forbidden to certain classes of society. The Chinese visitor, I Ching wrote that onions were forbidden because they caused pain, spoilt the eyesight and weakened the body. Even today these are not used in traditional Bania and Jain cuisine, which is probably the only Delhi food that has remained unchanged to this day.

During the Rajput rule of Delhi meat made a comeback on the

menu. It received greater emphasis with the arrival of the Afghans, Turks and other Central Asian people. Muslim cuisine on the Indian subcontinent is very different from that of any other Muslim nation. It is obvious that local influences such as cooking practices and the availability of a vast range of ingredients played an important role in its development. Onions and garlic were again in use to flavour the rich meat dishes, pulaos and biryanis that were part of this cuisine. Nuts and raisins were also used extensively, both in savoury dishes and in milk sweets and halvas. The Muslims also brought the concept of community eating to the rather austere eating habits of the time.

Ibn Batuta describes at length the dining customs of the Delhi Sultans. The dinners were formal with a fixed seating arrangement. It is interesting to note that judges, orators and jurists were the most honoured and sat at the head of the dining carpet, the Sultan's relatives and nobles followed and the common people were 'below the salt'. Before dinner the guests bowed to the Sultan or his representative and then sat at their appointed places. A rose flavoured sherbet was first served to all the guests. The meal which followed would consist of meat cooked in ghee flavoured with ginger and onion, naan, samosa filled with meat and spices, rice, fowl and halva. After the meal a barley drink would be served, followed by paan.

The dinners could be both private and public. The private dinners to which the nobles and others of high position were invited, were attended by the Sultan—it was said that by being in the Sultan's company the nobles would keep out of mischief! The public dinners were presided over by the palace officers but followed the same formal pattern as the private ones.

When Babar came to India he discovered that 'the dusty plains of Hindustan' did not produce the fruits that he loved. He imported grapes and melons and started their cultivation in India. By the time of Akbar these were plentiful in Delhi markets and the price lists of that time in the *Ain-I-Akbari* mention them along with indigenous fruit like mangoes, oranges, guavas, figs, plantains, mulberry, custard-apples, along with pomegranates and pineapple.

Other exotic spices and foods were brought by the Europeans and the food that evolved acquired new flavours. Chillies, for example were a late entrant to India. In the *Ain-I-Akbari* chillies are not mentioned as an ingredient in any of the recipes. It is said that the use of chillies in Delhi was recommended by Hakim Alvi, physician to Mohammed Shah Rangila to ward off the 'ill humours' thought to be generated by the canal flowing through Chandni Chowk.

All these influences married to the existing food culture resulted in a rich and varied cuisine. Eating became serious business and a good cook was jealously guarded. Kayasth food, particularly that of the Mathurs has borrowed heavily from the Muslim tradition, along with the language and culture.

The Partition saw many new influences flooding Delhi. Tandoori food from Central Asia came to the frontier and thence to Delhi. The man responsible for introducing this fare to Delhi was Kundan Lal of Moti Mahal Restaurant at Daryaganj. This remarkable man with a handlebar moustache started the legendry tandoori cuisine with only tandoori chicken. It was said of him that he educated the foreigner to eat with his fingers. Not many people know that the ubiquitious butter chicken was his innovation as was chicken pakora. Even at the height of his success he personally supervised his restaurant and kept a sharp eye on each table.

Today in Delhi you can get everything from pizza to paella, dosa, idli, dhokla with Thai, Mexican and Chinese food thrown in. 'Cho meen' has become an Indian dish and jostles for space with tandoori chicken and tikka kababs at roadside stalls.

So what exactly is Delhi Food? To find out, take a walk through the old city. All the traditional foods are available—from piste ki lauz and badaam ki lauz at Ghantewala and Kunwar Sain to habshi halwa at Ballimaran; from rabri and khurchan at Parathewali Gali (in addition to paranthas) to jalebi at the corner of Dariba and Chandni Chowk and Sultan ke kulle at Nai Sarak. At Jama Masjid there are a number of stalls selling foodstuff, both cooked and raw. You can eat kababs, biryani, kheer, kulfi, nankhatais and biscuits. Or you can go to Karim's or Jawahar Restaurant for a proper meal of korma, parsindas, bheja and a variety of rotis and naans.

But of course the best food from any region is to be found in the homes of the people. Each family has its own way of cooking a particular dish and each one is 'authentic'. Cookery is not a static art, ingredients are added or subtracted along the way according to individual tastes and whims and sometimes even by accident!

An important role in the evolution of cooking has been played by the joint family system. With many hands available, a great deal of care, effort and time went into the preparation of food and elaborate recipes were developed.

K.T. Achaya's *A Historical Dictionary of Indian Food* and *Indian Food: A Historical Companion* as well as Maheshwar

Dayal's *Rediscovering Delhi: The Story of Shahjahanabad* have been invaluable sources of information in the course of my research.

I am grateful to all the people who have given me their recipes. I am particularly indebted to Mrs. Zakia Zaheer for taking the time and trouble to read to me from her collection of old Urdu recipe books. One of these is called *Rezia ka Shahi Dastarkhwana* and another is a hundred-and-fifty year old treasure called *Pukht-o-Paaz Shehzada Mirza Mohommed Baker Ali Khan Sahib Bahadur ke Daroga Bawarchi, Janab Shiekh Ahmed Ali Sahib ka.* The latter is a mine of wonderful recipes and tips on cooking and eating. We are told how to salt fish, how to keep eggs fresh underground for up to one month, and there is even a method for tenderizing fish bones.

We are advised to eat only as much as will leave place for 'hava aur pani'—'air and water' not quite conveying the same thing. And we are informed that it takes at least three hours to digest a meal. There is also a warning against excessive medication.

The book mentions a way of making sugared almonds which 'the Englishman will never be able to copy, no matter how hard he tries. It would take one man one day to make half a seer of these'. The method described involves dipping ones fingers into hot sugar syrup and coating one almond at a time. When the sugar dries, the process is repeated several times till each almond appears as if it is coated with poppy seed. Not surprisingly, Sheikh Ahmed Ali tells us that 'not everyone can make this sweet as the fingers are bound to get burnt and blistered, and the shoulders will ache'. One can only marvel at the perseverence of those dedicated souls who actually made these almonds!

The book also has sample menus for feasts, both elaborate and ordinary. A special feast would consist of:

Pulao, five kinds—saffron biryani, chicken pulao, fish pulao, muzaafar pulao and muthanjan pulao.

Kababs, five kinds—chicken, fish, partridge, quail and duck. (The kababs in this context do not mean chicken tikka etc. which came from the frontier, but chicken, fish etc. cooked in dry masala. These were called 'gazak' and were had with drinks.)

Saalan (mutton), five kinds—shabdeg, korma, badaam saalan, fried arvi saalan and fried potato saalan.

Sweet, five kinds—shahi tukra, gulathi, phirni, lauz and jalebi.

Pakwan (fried bread), five kinds—plain poori, stuffed poori, plain samosa, layered samosa and gauja.

Naan, five kinds—taftan naan, sheermal, bakarkhani, salty layered parantha and sweet layered parantha.

In addition there would be curd, pickle, preserves and balai (top of milk).

A total of thirty-four kinds of food for each person. The book says that although even rich people cannot eat such a large quantity of food, it should be cooked as it will not go waste! Presumably it was distributed among less fortunate souls after the rich had had their fill.

The ordinary feast consisted of kofta, pulao, muzaafar, makhana (lotus seed) saalan, fried potato saalan, fried arvi saalan, kabab, shami kabab, phirni, poori and chapati. In all, ten kinds of food for each person. A meal such as this for ten persons cost the princely sum of four and a half rupees.

Food and festivities go together and this is especially true of weddings. Every family had its favourite bawarchi who would be called to make the pulao, biryani, roghanjosh, kofta et al. Halwais would arrive several days before the wedding and prepare vast quantities of laddoos, mithai, mathri, kachori and samosas which were stored for future use. Large circles of pastry called pakwan were pricked and crimped into elaborate patterns and then fried golden. They were fifteen to twenty inches across and frying them without breaking the pastry was an art in itself.

Amongst the Banias there was a ceremony to mark the installation of the karaha—the place where the halwais were to cook. The utensils used by the halwais were ceremoniously honoured to ensure that the food produced was wholesome and plentiful. Salt was ground in the grinding stone as an auspicious start to the proceedings. After this the halwais could get on with their work. These halwais and their associates—there could be up to fifteen or twenty of them—had to be fed and naturally could not be expected to cook for themselves. Whilst they churned out goodies for the wedding, the ladies of the house were busy cooking meals for them!

After the wedding, when the bride and groom came back for the ritual first visit to the bride's home, the new son-in-law was asked to kick away the fireplace of the halwais to mark the end of ceremonies.

With life-styles having changed, the hustle-bustle of cooks and halwais has been replaced by the convenient caterer. Wedding food tastes much the same everywhere, with a bewildering variety of cuisines to choose from.

We seem to have become very sophisticated, and gone are the simple joys of watching halwais at work and tasting laddoos and mathris straight off the fire.

The Muslims have a feast only for women one day before the wedding. The daughters-in-law of the family dress in all their finery and serve the food to the guests.

The bride is dressed by seven suhagans (married women) in seven items of jewellery made with flowers. At the wedding itself she does not come out till the nikah (wedding ceremony) is complete. The groom is supposed to to see her for the first time at a ceremony called aarsi musaf. Aarsi is actually a ring worn on the thumb with a mirror on it instead of a gemstone. An ordinary mirror can be used instead. The bride and groom sit side by side and are covered with a dupatta; a copy of the Koran and a mirror is placed between them. The groom reads a few lines from the Koran and looks at the bride's face in the mirror.

When the couple visits the bride's home for the first time after the wedding, she takes with her seven types of fruit and seven types of vegetables. The couple hit each other with flowers—this is called playing chauthi. The bride's mother gives her a set of clothes called the chauthi ka jora.

Rituals associated with birth are very similar in all communities. A thanksgiving ceremony is performed at the completion of the seventh month of pregnancy. The girl's mother sends sweets and clothes and these are given to her in the gode bharai (literally, filling the lap) as a blessing for the well being of the mother and the unborn child. After the birth of the child the mother and child are supposed to be isolated for six days. (This is rarely done now except perhaps in very othodox families.) The ceremony to mark the end of this isolation is called chhati. Often this coincides with the naming of the child. The maternal grandparents of the child send clothes for the child and the parents. Among Banias the new mother comes out of her room wearing the barber's shoes.

Indeed the nai or barber played a very important role among all the communities in Delhi. He was aware of all that went on in each house and conveyed the gossip from place to place. He played the role of matchmaker, was sent with the invitations to marriages and hair cutting seems to have been quite incidental! The nain bahu or barber's wife was present at all the wedding ceremonies and was given the clothes worn by the bride on the morning before the wedding.

Of course the nai really came into his own at the sirkaaj or shaving of the child's head. (The Muslims call this ceremony akika.) In all communities the maternal grandparents of the child send clothes and sweets, and the paternal grandparents host a lavish feast. Among Muslims one goat is sacrificed for the akika of a girl and two for that of a boy. The meat of these animals is not eaten by the grandparents but is distributed among the relatives.

The Khatris have a quaint custom called russa mani. Before the child's sirkaaj, the mother sulks and goes to her parents' house. Her in-laws come with gifts and clothes and persuade her to come back for the ceremony.

In addition to these ceremonies there are major festivals like Holi, Diwali, Id and a host of minor ones throughout the year when family and friends forgather to eat and drink and special food is prepared.

There are many communities living in Delhi today whose cuisine is as rich and varied as anything included in this book. However, the recipes which follow are taken from the cuisine of the Muslims, Kayasths, Banias and Khatris. These were the four main groups of people who settled in Shahjehanabad, which became Delhi.

Soups are not part of Delhi cuisine. Kababs, liver, dry chicken and fish were served with drinks and were called gazak. 'Gazak Daaru' was a must before the more serious business of dinner began. The meal (with the exception of the sweet) was served either on a metal thali or on a pattal—a platter made of dried leaves stitched together.

Among the Muslims and Kayasths the main items on the menu were the meat dishes—all the others were there to complement the meal! I therefore thought it was only fitting to begin this book with a chapter on meat.

MEASUREMENTS

I have used kilograms (kg) and grams (gm) in all recipes, but there are also teaspoons (tsp) and tablespoons (tbsp). I have also used the terms 'pinch' and 'handful' in some cases.

Cup measures have also been given in brackets for those who do not have weighing scales, except where the quantities used are large.

1 tsp = 5 gm/ml
1 tbsp = 3 tsp
1 cup = 8 oz or 225 ml/gm
450 ml = 1 pint
1 kg = 2.2 lbs

COOKING MEDIUM

I have used ghee (vanaspati) for most recipes. Any cooking oil can be substituted unless otherwise indicated. Bania cuisine uses either pure ghee or mustard oil.

To make mustard oil ready for use:

Heat 2 kg mustard oil till smoking. Turn off heat and throw in 1 tbsp salt water. The oil will crackle. Cool completely, bottle and use.

SPICES

Freshly ground spices give best results, but when pressed for time you can use:

1 tsp ginger paste for 1 inch piece of ginger

1 tsp garlic paste for 5-6 cloves garlic

KACHRI

Kachri is a summer fruit which looks like a miniature melon. When dried it is used in chutneys and also to flavour and tenderise mutton. I have used it in quite a few recipes.

DUM

The process of dum is used quite often in Indian cooking. When a coal fire is used for cooking, the pan is sealed using dough made with flour and water and put on a very low fire with live coals on the lid so that the pan is heated from above and below. On a gas ring this can be achieved by placing the sealed pan on the lowest possible flame and putting a pan of hot water on the lid. Keep replacing the water as it cools with more hot water. The pan can also be put in a low oven, 150°C (300°F).

TO SKIN TOMATOES

I have used skinned tomatoes in most recipes. To skin tomatoes put them in a bowl and pour in boiling water to cover. Cover and leave for one minute. Drain and plunge into cold water. The skins come off quite easily.

GARAM MASALA

Most recipes require garam masala. The packaged variety is not really satisfactory and it is well worth the effort to make your own.

3 tsp black peppercorn
3 tsp cumin seeds
20 cloves
5 bay leaves, crushed
Good pinch mace flakes
Seeds of 5 black cardamoms
Seeds of 20 green cardamoms
3 inch piece cinnamon
1 nutmeg

Separately roast the first five ingredients on a hot griddle. Cool and grind with cardamom seeds, cinnamon and nutmeg. (These three are not roasted as they turn bitter.) Sieve and store in an airtight container.

Make small quantities of garam masala at a time as it loses its flavour if kept too long.

Mutton

Mutton refers to goat meat throughtout the book. Cooking times for mutton are approximate as they depend upon the quality of the meat. Try and choose meat that is pink rather than red—the redder the meat, the older the animal and the longer it will take to cook. Remove all visible fat from the mutton and wash thoroughly in running water to remove small pieces of bone and hair.

SHABDEG
Mince Ball Curry with Kidney,
Brain and Turnips

Serves: 10-12

This rich combination of koftas, kidneys, brain, turnips and potatoes was traditionally cooked overnight on charcoal embers. Shab means night and deg refers to the cooking pot. This adaptation of an old family recipe is made on a gas stove and takes much less time.

Kofta:

1 kg mutton, very finely minced
750 gm (6 large) onions
300 gm (1½ cups) ghee
1 inch piece ginger
10–12 cloves garlic
25 gm (1½ tbsp) poppy seeds, soaked and drained
1 green chilli
50 gm (3 heaped tbsp) parched gram, ground and sieved
2 level tsp garam masala powder

1 tsp salt
2 tbsp chopped fresh coriander
2 eggs

Masala:

250 gm (2 large) onions, minced
1 inch piece ginger, ground
10-12 cloves garlic, ground
2 tsp salt
1 tsp powdered red chilli
2 tsp powdered coriander seeds
1 tsp turmeric powder
3 tsp garam masala powder
1 tsp pure ghee or butter
250 gm (2 cups) curd
500 gm (6 large) tomatoes, skinned and chopped

Shabdeg:

6 turnips, even sized
12 potatoes, even sized
125 gm (1¼ cups) ghee
6 kidneys, cleaned and halved
250 gm (2 cups) curd
4 sheep's brains (membranes removed)
½ tsp turmeric powder
3 medium onions, sliced
3 medium tomatoes, skinned and chopped
½ tsp salt
½ tsp garam masala powder
2 tsp chopped fresh coriander
2–3 drops kewra essence

Kofta mixture: Slice onions finely and fry in hot ghee till golden brown.

Grind together ginger, garlic, poppy seeds and green chilli. Mix into mince along with remaining ingredients and one third fried onions. Keep aside.

Masala: Place remaining fried onions back on heat, stir in minced onions and fry for 2-3 minutes. Add next eight ingredients. Continue to stir and cook, adding curd a little at a time. Stir in tomatoes and cook till ghee separates and masala becomes paste-like. Remove from heat.

Stir 2 tbsp masala into mince. Beat thoroughly with your hand till it feels light. Using greased hands, form mince into largish koftas and keep aside.

To the masala in the pan, add one litre water and bring to boil. Gently put in koftas. Reduce heat and cook uncovered for 10 minutes. Cover and cook for a further 30 minutes.

Shabdeg: Peel turnips and potatoes, trim to size of koftas, prick all over, then fry in ghee till pink. Put potatoes, turnips and kidneys into pan with koftas. Whip curd and pour on top. Shake pan gently to combine. Add 250 ml warm water, cover, seal pan and put on lowest possible heat for one hour.

Put ½ tsp turmeric into 1½ litres water with brains and bring to boil. Drain, cool and cut into 4 pieces each. Keep aside. In the ghee left over from frying turnips and potatoes, fry sliced onion till golden. Add tomatoes, salt and garam masala. Fry for 5 minutes. Carefully turn brains into masala and cook for 5 minutes.

Uncover pan of Shabdeg, stir in cooked brains and kewra essence. Garnish with chopped fresh coriander and serve with roti or bakarkhani.

RAAN
Roast Leg of Lamb

Serves: 10-12

The unique flavour of this raan comes from dry roasting the spices and adding them at the end of the cooking process along with roasted parched gram.

The original family recipe used a smaller quantity of curd and more of the gram and spices. This resulted in a dry roast leg that could be carried on journeys as it could be kept for a long time without going 'off'. I have used a little more curd and a smaller quantity of gram to make a thick masala gravy; the taste remains the same.

1 leg of mutton 2–2½ kg

Marinade:

100 gm dried kachri or 2 inch piece raw papaya
6 dried figs
300 gm (5 medium) onions
100 gm (approx. 4 medium pods) garlic
½ nutmeg, grated
Pinch mace flakes
1½ tsp salt

Dry masala:

200 gm cumin seeds
100 gm black peppercorn
100 gm aniseed (saunf)
100 gm coriander seeds
100 gm whole black cardamom, seeds only

Raan:

500 gm (2½ cups) ghee
300 gm (5 medium) onions, sliced

Mutton

200 gm (2 cups) parched gram (chana), roasted, ground and sieved
1 kg curd, whipped

Garnish:

250 gm (1¼ cups) ghee
300 gm (5 medium) onions, sliced
4 large potatoes, peeled and coarsely grated
25 gm (1 tbsp) almonds, blanched and slivered
25 gm (1 tbsp) sultanas, cleaned

Mutton: Clean mutton and prick all over with a fork.

Soak kachri and figs for 4-5 hours. (There is no need to soak papaya, if using). Drain. Grind with onion, garlic, nutmeg, mace and salt. Rub marinade all over mutton and refrigerate overnight.

Dry masala: Separately roast each spice except cardamom seeds on griddle. Cool, grind very fine and sieve. Grind and sieve cardamom seeds. Mix with other spices. Keep aside. (This can be done a few days ahead of time and stored in an airtight container).

Raan: Heat half the ghee in a large heavy based pan. Put in mutton along with marinade and cook on medium heat, turning mutton till light brown on all sides. Reduce heat, cover and cook for 2–2½ hours. Do not add any water but turn mutton from time to time, scraping any masala sticking to bottom of pan.

In a separate pan heat remaining ghee and fry sliced onions till golden.

When meat is tender add curd, gram and fried onions. Cook for a few minutes and add previously prepared dry masala. Gently lift raan to allow masala to coat it on all sides. Cover and leave on very low heat for 15–20 minutes.

Garnish: Fry sliced onions in ghee till golden. Drain and keep aside. Fry potatoes till crisp and golden. Mix onions, potatoes, almonds and sultanas.

Place raan on a large platter and sprinkle with garnish.

Excellent served with parantha.

ROGHANJOSH
Thick Mutton Curry

Serves: 6-8

Special Muslim cooks were often called by Delhi families to make the meat preparations for large parties. My mother once asked one of these cooks for his recipe for Roghanjosh. 'Madam', he replied, 'Ask your husband to teach me the law and I will certainly teach you to make this meat'.

Of course she had to get the recipe from somewhere else!

Roghan means ghee and *Josh* is the term for boiling—literally cooked in ghee!

1 kg mutton pieces
2-3 dried red chillies, soaked in water for ½ hour
Seeds of 6 green cardamoms
12-15 cloves
3 tsp powdered coriander seeds
20 cloves garlic, peeled
2 inch piece ginger
2 tsp poppy seeds
1½ tsp cumin seeds
½ nutmeg, grated
Pinch mace flakes
½ tsp turmeric powder
350 gm (1¾ cups) ghee
125 gm (2 medium) onions, minced
125 gm (1 cup) curd
100 gm (2 medium) tomatoes, skinned and chopped
2 tsp salt
1 tsp garam masala powder
Chopped fresh coriander

Wash and dry mutton. Drain chillies and grind along with next ten ingredients. Keep aside.

Heat ghee and fry onion till golden. Stir in ground masala paste and cook, adding curd a little at a time. Add tomatoes and salt and cook for a further 5 minutes. Add meat and cook, stirring till rich brown. Pour in 300 ml warm water. Reduce heat, cover and cook for one hour or till tender. Sprinkle with garam masala and fresh coriander.

Serve with bakarkhani or roti.

MUTTON KORMA
Mutton Curry

Serves: 6-8

1 kg mutton pieces
50 gm (2 pods) garlic
2 inch piece ginger
2 tsp salt
200 gm (3 medium) onions
1½ tbsp poppy seeds
50 gm (⅓ cup) almonds, blanched
6 tbsp coriander seeds, lightly roasted
10 cloves
Seeds of 8-10 green cardamoms
1 inch piece cinnamon
200 gm (1 cup) ghee
200 gm (1½ cups) curd, whipped
2-3 drops kewra essence
Chopped fresh coriander to garnish

Wash and dry mutton. Grind garlic and ginger with salt and marinate mutton in this for about 2 hours. Slice 150 gms onions and keep aside. Grind remaining onion with next 6 ingredients.

Heat ghee and fry sliced onions till golden. Remove with slotted spoon and set aside. Put ground masala into the same ghee and fry for 2-3 minutes. Add marinated meat and cook till liquid dries. Pour in 250 ml warm water, cover and simmer on low heat for about one hour, stirring occasionally, till meat is almost done. Grind fried onions and add to meat along with curd. Cover and cook for a further 15-20 minutes. Stir in kewra essence. Garnish with fresh coriander, and serve with roti or parantha.

KORMA DILPASAND
Mutton Curry

Serves: 6-8

1 kg mutton pieces
3-4 pieces cinnamon, 1 inch each
2 bay leaves
8 green cardamoms
10-12 cloves
½ tsp black peppercorn
Large pinch mace flakes
250 gm (4 medium) onions
15 cloves garlic
2 inch piece ginger
2 heaped tbsp coriander seeds
2 whole dried red chillies
200 gm (1 cup) ghee
2 tsp salt
250 gm (2 cups) curd
1 tsp garam masala powder

Clean mutton and put into pan with next six ingredients. Cover with water, bring to boil, reduce heat and simmer for half an hour.

Grind one third onions with ginger, garlic, coriander seeds and red chillies. Finely slice remaining onions. Heat ghee and fry sliced onions till golden. Drain and keep aside. Put ground masala into ghee and fry for 1-2 minutes. Drain meat and discard whole spices. Put meat into masala along with cooking water, curd and salt. Crush fried onions and stir into meat with garam masala. Cover and cook on low heat, stirring occasionally for 30 minutes or till meat is tender.

Serve with roti.

DO PIAZA-1
Mutton Curry with Onions
Serves: 6-8

Do Piaza was described by Edward Terry, chaplain to Sir Thomas Roe as 'the most savoury meat I have ever tasted, and do almost think it is the very dish that Jacob made ready for his father when he got the blessing'.

The recipe in the *Ain-I-Akbari* is for 10s.meat that is middling fat, 2s. ghi, 2s. onions, ¼ s. salt ⅛s. fresh pepper, 1d. each of cumin seed, coriander seed, cardamom and cloves, and 2d. pepper. Where 's' is seer or approximately 1 kg and 'd' is dam which is roughly equal to 20 gm.

The 'fresh pepper' referred to is obviously an error as the word 'fresh' in every other recipe occurs before 'ginger' and as chillies (which might have been indicated by the words) have not been used in any of the recipes, I have assumed that ginger was the ingredient used. Also the quantity of salt seems excessive by modern standards—¼ seer would be 250 gm and reduced to a tenth would be 25 gm or 5 teaspoons!

Reducing the proportions to one tenth one gets the following recipe:

1 kg mutton pieces
200 gm (1 cup) ghee
200 gm (3 medium) onions, sliced
1 inch piece ginger, finely chopped
2 tsp salt
1½ tsp cumin seeds
3 tsp coriander seeds

27

1 tsp black peppercorn
1 tsp cloves
15 green cardamoms

Wash mutton. Heat ghee in a pan and fry onions golden. Add ginger and fry for 1-2 minutes. Add mutton and cook till liquid dries and meat is browned.

Dry roast separately cumin, coriander, peppercorns and cloves and grind. Add to meat along with salt and cardamoms. Pour in 500 ml water, cover and cook on low heat for one and a half hours till meat is tender.

This is a fairly simple recipe and gives a nice 'ordinary' meat curry.

DO PIAZA-2
Mutton Curry with Onions

Serves: 6-8

Over the years the Do Piaza has evolved and there are several versions that are made, everyone having their own favourite recipe. Some people use double the proportion of onions to meat and some use only two onions.

My grandmother made the following version of Do Piaza using equal quantities of meat and onions.

1 kg mutton pieces
250 gm (1¼ cups) ghee
1 kg onions, half sliced and half ground
2 inch piece ginger, ground
12-15 cloves garlic, ground
2-3 tsp salt
500 gm (4 cups) curd, whipped
2 tsp cumin seeds, roasted and ground
4 tsp coriander seeds, roasted and ground
10-12 whole green cardamoms, crushed
1 tsp garam masala powder
2-3 drops kewra essence
Chopped fresh coriander

Heat ghee in a pan and fry sliced onions till golden. Remove onions, drain, crush and keep aside.

In the same pan fry ground onions till beginning to colour, add ginger and garlic and cook for one minute. Add mutton and salt and cook for 10 minutes. Put in curd, crushed onions, cumin, coriander powder, cardamoms and garam masala. Pour in 250 ml water, cover and cook for one hour or till meat is tender. Stir in kewra essence. Garnish with chopped coriander.

Serve with roti or naan.

(There is quite a lot of ghee in this recipe. After the meat is cooked, allow it to stand for 15-20 minutes and skim off the extra ghee from the surface).

KHARE MASALE KA GOSHT
Mutton Cooked with Whole Spices

Serves: 6-8

1 kg mutton pieces
200 gm (1 cup) ghee
250 gm (2 large) onions, sliced
30-35 cloves garlic, sliced lengthwise
3 inch piece ginger, cut into thin strips
2 bay leaves
4 black cardamoms
½ tsp black peppercorn
1 tbsp cumin seeds
1 tbsp coriander seeds
10 cloves
8 green cardamoms
2 pieces cinnamon, 1 inch each
1½ tsp salt
300 gm (6 medium) tomatoes, skinned and chopped
250 gm (2 cups) curd, whipped

Heat ghee and fry sliced onions till golden, add garlic and ginger, stir and cook for 1-2 minutes. Add all spices and fry for one minute. Pour in 250 ml water and salt, cover and cook for 5 minutes. Stir in tomatoes and cook for a further 5-10 minutes till mixture is paste-like. Add meat and curd, cover and cook on low heat, stirring occasionally, for 1½ hours or till meat is tender. Add more water during cooking if necessary.

SAFRI GOSHT
White Mutton Curry

Serves: 6-8

This meat is cooked with whole spices and the appearance remains white.

1 kg mutton pieces
100 gm (½ cup) ghee
250 gm button onions, peeled
1½ tsp cumin seeds
1 tsp black peppercorn
6 black cardamoms
6 green cardamoms
4 pieces cinnamon, 1 inch each
1 tsp cloves
4 bay leaves
2-3 dried whole red chillies
1½ tsp salt
500 gm (4 cups) curd

Heat ghee in a pan and fry button onions for 2-3 minutes till slightly pink, drain and keep aside.

Put all spices and red chillies into the same pan and fry for 1-2 minutes. Add meat and cook for 5-10 minutes. Pour in 300 ml water, reduce heat, cover and cook for one hour. Stir in curd and salt and cook for 30 minutes till meat is tender. Add reserved button onions and cook for a further 10 minutes.

Serve with roti.

BABU SHAHI'S KUNDAN KALIA
White Mutton

Serves: 6-8

Babu Shahi Bawarchi of Matka Pir comes from a long line of specialist cooks. His ancestors worked in the kitchens of the Emperor Shahjehan, which is why they are referred to as Shahi Bawarchis. He and his older brother, Boobi used to cook for well-to-do Delhi families. Now he caters from his establishment at Matka Pir. Babu remembers the time when butter-balls were sold in Jama Masjid at the rate of two butter-balls for one paisa. 'Some people would eat the butter, some would rub it on their heads, some on their hands and face' he says. He also recalls the fairs in Nizamuddin and at Humayun's Tomb where, in addition to cockfights, there were partridge fights, quail fights, kite flying. Young men would oil their bodies and show off their muscles before jumping into the tank at the shrine of Hazrat Nizamuddin.

1 kg mutton pieces
250 gm (2 cups) curd
6 whole green chillies
4 tbsp ghee
10 green cardamoms
8 cloves
2 bay leaves
300 ml milk
4 level tbsp desiccated coconut
2 tsp salt

Wash mutton and keep aside.

Whip curd and put into a pan with green chillies. Stir over moderate heat just till boiling. (Do not worry if it curdles). Remove from heat and keep aside.

Heat ghee in a pan and fry cardamoms, cloves and bay leaves for 1-2 minutes. Add mutton, stir and cook for 3-5 minutes. Reduce heat and add milk and coconut. Cover and cook on low heat for 1-1½ hours. Strain curd into meat, discarding chillies. Add 250 ml water and salt. Cook for 15-20 minutes till meat is tender.

MUTTON ISTOO
Mutton Stew

Serves: 6-8

A recipe from *Rezia ka Shahi Dastarkhwana.*

1 kg mutton pieces
1 kg onions, sliced
2 inch piece ginger, finely sliced
20 cloves garlic, sliced lengthwise
12 whole dried red chillies
½ tsp cloves
8-10 green cardamoms
250 gm (2 cups) curd
250 gm (1¼ cups) ghee
1½ tsp salt

Wash and clean mutton. Mix in a pan with remaining ingredients. Cover and cook on low heat for 2–2½ hours till meat is tender.

DAHI AUR DHUYE KA GOSHT
Smoked Mutton, Cooked with Curd

Serves: 4-5

A recipe from *Rezia ka Shahi Dastarkhwana*

500 gm mutton pieces
250 gm (4 medium) onions
12-15 cloves garlic, ground
2 inch piece ginger, finely sliced
Pinch powdered red chilli
2 tbsp powdered coriander seeds
1½ tsp salt
200 gm (1 cup) ghee
500 gm (4 cups) thick curd
2 tbsp chopped mint leaves
3-4 green chillies, seeded and chopped
½ tsp salt
2-3 small pieces charcoal

Put meat in a pan with 2 sliced onions, garlic, ginger, red chilli, coriander and 1½ tsp salt. Add 250 ml water, cover and cook on low heat for 1½ hours or till meat is tender.

Add ghee, stir and cook till well browned. Remove from fire and keep aside.

Slice remaining onions very fine. Mix with mint, green chillies and ½ tsp salt.

Whip curd. (Tie curd in muslin and hang for half an hour if it is not thick enough.)

Cover meat in the pan, with one third curd and top with one third onions, then another third curd and so on.

Place a piece foil or onion skin on top. Heat coal till red hot, place on foil and sprinkle with a few drops of water. Immediately cover pan as tightly as possible and leave for 15-20 minutes on very low heat. When serving, try and keep the layers of meat, curd and onions intact.

DAL GOSHT
Mutton with Lentils

Serves: 6-8

A recipe from *Rezia ka Shahi Dastarkhwana*.

250 gm (1¼ cups) Bengal gram (chana dal)
500 gm mutton pieces
125 gm (2 medium) onions, sliced
20-25 cloves garlic, ground
1 tsp salt
½ tsp turmeric powder
Pinch pepper
200 gm (1 cup) ghee
2 inch piece ginger, finely sliced
2-3 green chillies, chopped
2 tbsp chopped fresh coriander
½ tsp garam masala powder

Wash dal and soak in water for 3-4 hours.

Clean and wash meat, put into a pan with onions, garlic, salt, turmeric and pepper. Cook on low heat till liquid dries. Add ghee and cook, stirring till brown. Drain dal and add to meat with ginger. Pour in one litre water and cook, stirring occasionally, till meat and dal are tender. Stir in green chillies, coriander and garam masala.

ALU KA SAALAN
Mutton with Potatoes

Serves: 6-8

A recipe from the *Pukht-o-Paaz.*

500 gm mutton pieces
125 gm (⅔ cup) ghee
200 gm (3 medium) onions, half sliced and half minced
15-20 cloves garlic, ground
1 inch piece ginger, ground
2 tsp powdered coriander seeds
½ tsp turmeric powder
200 gm (1½ cups) curd
2 tsp salt
1 tsp garam masala powder
1 kg medium sized potatoes

Wash and dry mutton. Heat ghee in a pan and fry sliced onions till golden. Drain and keep aside. Add minced onions to pan and fry till pale gold. Stir in garlic, ginger, coriander and turmeric and cook, adding one or two tbsp curd till masala is brown and ghee separates. Add meat and salt and cook, stirring occasionally, till liquid dries and meat is browned. Add remaining curd, garam masala and 500 ml water. Cook covered for 45 minutes or till meat is almost done. Peel and quarter potatoes and add to meat, adding more water if necessary. Cover and cook for a further 30 minutes till meat and potatoes are tender.

Variations:
Tale Alu ka Saalan: Fry the potatoes before adding to meat.

Shalgam ka Saalan: Peel and halve one kg small turnips, fry till pink and add to meat.

Makhane ka Saalan: Fry 250 gm lotus seeds in 100 gm (½ cup) ghee till golden, add to mutton and cook on low heat for 30 minutes.

BADAM PARSINDE
Parsinda with Almonds

Serves: 8-10

Parsinde, also called pasanda, are pieces of meat cut from the leg or shoulder, and flattened by beating and scoring with a knife. This way of preparing meat originated in Delhi although now you can get them all over the country.

1½ kg parsindas

Marinade:

3 medium onions
20 cloves garlic
2 inch piece ginger
3 dried kachri, soaked in water or 1 inch piece raw papaya
3 dried figs, soaked in water
3 tsp poppy seeds
25 almonds, blanched

Gravy:

250 gm (1¼ cups) ghee
750 gm (6 large) onions, finely sliced
2 inch piece ginger, chopped
10 cloves garlic, ground
2 bay leaves
2 inch piece cinnamon
8 green cardamoms
Seeds of 4 black cardamoms, powdered
2 tsp salt
3 tbsp powdered coriander seeds
1 tsp garam masala powder
1 tsp powdered red chilli
250 gm (2 cups) curd
250 gm (3 large) tomatoes, skinned and chopped
Pinch saffron

Garnish:

Wash and dry parsindas. Grind together all ingredients for marinade, rub well over meat and leave for 4 hours.

Heat ghee in a frying pan and fry onions till golden. Stir in 2 tsp water. Add ginger, garlic, bay leaves, cinnamon, green cardamoms and powdered black cardamom. Fry for 1-2 minutes. Add salt, coriander powder, garam masala and chilli. Stir and cook, adding a little water till ghee separates. Put in meat along with marinade. Cover and cook on low heat for one hour. Shake pan from time to time. Whip curd and strain into meat along with tomatoes. Cook till meat is tender. Dissolve saffron in a little hot water and stir into meat.

Garnish with split almonds and chopped fresh coriander. Serve with bakarkhani, roti or rice.

BHARVA PARSINDE
Stuffed Parsinda

Serves: 6-8

Ask the butcher to cut large even sized pieces of parsinda for this very special dish.

1 kg parsindas

Filling:

50 gm (2½ inches) ginger
50 gm (⅓ cup) blanched almonds
Handful of fresh coriander
4-5 sprigs mint
4 hard boiled eggs
1 tsp salt
Juice of 1 lime

Gravy:

2 dried figs
4-5 dried kachri or 2 inch piece raw papaya
50 gm (6 tbsp) poppy seeds
50 gm (2 pods) garlic
50 gm (2½ inches) ginger
250 gm (1¼ cups) ghee
500 gm (4 large) onions, finely sliced
1 tsp powdered red chilli
1½ tsp turmeric powder
2 tsp salt
3 tsp powdered coriander seeds
250 gm (2 cups) curd
250 gm (3 large) tomatoes, skinned and chopped
6 green cardamoms
1 tsp garam masala powder
Chopped fresh coriander to garnish

Filling: Finely chop ginger, almonds, coriander, mint and eggs. Mix in salt and lime juice. Put a little filling in the centre of each parsinda, roll to enclose filling and tie with string. Keep aside.

Gravy: Soak figs and kachri for 1-2 hours, (there is no need to soak papaya if used). Drain and grind with poppy seed, ginger and garlic.

Heat ghee in pan and fry sliced onions till golden. Remove with slotted spoon, grind and keep aside.

Stir in red chilli, turmeric, salt and coriander powder into ghee. Add ground masala paste, stir and cook adding 1-2 tsp curd. Add tomatoes and continue to cook till masala is a rich brown and the ghee separates. Add remaining curd and cardamoms. Put in stuffed parsindas and cook turning carefully, till liquid dries. Add ground, fried onions and 500 ml water. Cover and cook over low heat for one hour or till done. Shake the pan occasionally. Carefully remove string from parsindas. Garnish with garam masala and fresh coriander.

Serve with roti or bakarkhani.

Note: For easier handling you can allow the parsindas to cool completely, remove string and then reheat in an oven.

BHOORE PARSINDE
Dry Parsinda

Serves: 5-6

These parsindas are dry and light brown in appearance.

1 kg parsindas
250 gm (1¼ cups) ghee
1 kg onions, finely sliced
2 dried kachri, ground or 1 inch piece raw papaya, ground
2 tsp salt
2 inch piece ginger, ground
20 cloves garlic, ground
1 tsp powdered red chilli
2 tsp powdered coriander seeds
250 gm (2 cups) curd
125 gm (1¼ cups) roasted parched gram (channa)
1 tsp garam masala powder
Sprigs of mint and onion rings to garnish

Heat ghee in a frying pan and fry a quarter of the onions till golden. Add parsindas, kachri and salt. Cover and cook on low heat for 45 minutes till half done. Add remaining onions and cook till liquid dries. Add ginger, garlic, chilli and coriander and cook, adding curd a little at a time. Grind and sieve roasted gram and add to meat with garam masala. Cover and transfer to a slow oven, 150°C (300°F), for 10-15 minutes.

Serve garnished with mint and onion rings.

SOOKHE PARSINDE
Dry Parsinda

Serves: 10-12

This excellent recipe is from Mrs M.R.Chinoy of Bombay.

2 kg parsindas
200 gm garlic
2 inch piece ginger
4 tbsp lime juice
1½ tsp salt
Pinch powdered red chilli
3½ level tbsp poppy seeds
180 gm chironji
500 gm (4 cups) curd
2 tbsp ghee
Lime wedges and onion rings to garnish

Grind garlic and ginger, mix in lime juice, salt and red chilli. Rub well over meat. Leave to marinate for at least 4 hours.

Roast chironji and poppy seeds on griddle. Grind and mix into meat along with curd and ghee. Put into a shallow baking dish and cook in pre-heated oven 400°C (200°F) for one and a half hours. Reduce heat to 350°C (180°F) and cook for one hour more or till tender. Turn meat once or twice during baking.

Serve garnished with lime wedges and onion rings.

PARSINDE KI SEEKH
Parsinda Cooked on Skewers

Serves: 5-6

1 kg parsindas
2 dried figs
6 dried kachri (or 2 inch piece raw papaya)
5 tsp poppy seeds
250 gm (2 large) onions
20 cloves garlic
250 gm (2 cups) curd
1½ tsp salt
2 tsp ghee
Small piece of coal
1 tsp garam masala powder
½ tsp powdered red chilli
Onion rings and lime wedges to garnish

Soak figs and kachri for 4 hours, drain and grind with poppy seeds, onion and garlic (There is no need to soak papaya if used). Add salt and half the curd and mix into meat.

Put into a pan and make a depression in the centre. Put ghee into a piece of foil and place it in this depression. Hold coal with a pair of tongs in a flame till red hot. Place it into the ghee. Immediately cover as tightly as possible and leave meat to marinate for 4 hours.

Remove coal, strain ghee into meat and mix in garam masala and red chilli.

Wrap pieces of parsinda around skewers and tie in place with wet string.

Barbecue over charcoal, turning frequently till golden brown and tender.

Serve garnished with onion rings and lime wedges.

My grandmother used to wrap these parsindas around a pencil and cook them in a frying pan.

NEHARI
Mutton and Kofta Stew

Serves: 6-8

The word 'Nehari' means first thing in the morning. It is usually cooked at night (paye ki nehari is cooked overnight) and eaten next morning, particularly in the month of Ramzan.

This unusual recipe from the *Pukht-o-Paaz* is made with mutton, not trotters and includes koftas.

Kofta:
½ kg fine mince
1 medium onion, sliced and fried in 1 tbsp ghee till golden
2 tbsp roasted parched gram (channa), ground and sieved
1 tbsp chopped fresh coriander
100 gm (½ cup) ghee

Nehari:

500 gm mutton pieces with bone
250 gm wheat
100 gm (½ cup) rice
3 tbsp coriander seeds
6 tbsp ghee
2 medium onions, chopped
10-12 cloves garlic, ground
½ tsp cumin seeds
1 tsp salt
½ tsp turmeric powder
12-15 cloves
12 green cardamoms

Kofta: Mix all ingredients for kofta thoroughly. Form into walnut sized balls and fry lightly. Keep aside.

Nehari: Cook wheat in one litre water till one cup remains. (You could use 100 gm wheat porridge in one litre water and cook for 10 minutes). Strain through muslin, squeezing out as much liquid as possible. Repeat the process with rice, cooking it in 1½ litres water for 15 minutes. Discard wheat and rice and keep the liquids. You should have 500 ml altogether.

Grind coriander seeds with ¾ cup water, strain through muslin squeezing out all the liquid. Keep liquid aside and discard seeds.

Heat 4 tbsp ghee and fry onions till golden. Add mutton, garlic, cumin, turmeric and salt. Cook, adding coriander water a little at a time till liquid dries. Pour in reserved wheat and rice water and 500 ml warm water. In a separate pan heat remaining ghee and fry cloves and cardamoms for one minute. Add to mutton. Carefully put in koftas. Cover and seal pan with flour paste and cook on a tender fire for 3 hours.

Serve with naan or roti.

PAYE KI NEHARI
Trotter Stew

Serves: 4-5

A recipe from Mrs Zakia Zaheer.
This dish made with trotters was traditionally cooked overnight and had for breakfast. Most people now make it in a pressure cooker.

2 pairs sheep's trotters
200 gm (3 medium) onions
25 cloves garlic
3 tsp coriander seeds
2 dried red chillies
1 tsp salt
½ tsp turmeric powder
150 gm (¾ cup) ghee
200 gm (1½ cups) curd
2-3 green chillies, chopped
2 tbsp chopped fresh coriander
6 cloves
1 tsp garam masala powder

Put trotters into boiling water and clean thoroughly. Cut into pieces. (The butcher will usually do this for you).

Grind onions, garlic, coriander seeds and chillies. Mix in salt and turmeric. Heat 100 gms ghee in a pressure cooker and fry masala paste for 2-3 minutes. Put in trotters and 750 ml water and cook at 15lb pressure for 45 minutes.

Allow pressure to drop by itself. Cool slightly, then remove trotters. Using a marrow-spoon, take out all the marrow and stir into cooking liquid. Discard bones.

Stir and cook nehari for 5-10 minutes. Add whipped curd, green chillies and fresh coriander. Heat remaining ghee in a small pan, fry cloves and add to nehari with garam masala.

Note: For the traditional method put trotters in a large pan, cover with plenty of water and cook on low heat for 4-6 hours. (Keep checking during cooking and add more water if necessary.) Cool and proceed as above.

SIRI PAYE
Head and Trotter Stew

Serves: 6-8

This is a very nourishing stew and was recommended for people who needed 'to build up strength' after an illness!

Ask the butcher to skin, clean and cut the goat's head and clean and cut the trotters. Buy them the day before they are to be served. Keep the brain separately.

1 goat's head, cleaned and cut
2 pairs sheep trotters, cleaned and cut
1+1 tsp salt
4 dried kachri, ground or 2 inch piece raw papaya, ground
200 gm (1 cup) ghee
200 gm (3 medium) onions, slice half and grind half
1 inch piece ginger, ground
10 cloves garlic, ground
½ tsp turmeric powder
Pinch powdered red chilli
200 gm (1⅓ cups) curd
1 brain, with membranes removed, washed and cut into 4 pieces

Put head and trotters in a large pan with one tsp salt and kachri and cover with plenty of water. Bring to boil, reduce heat and simmer for 5-6 hours. (Check water during cooking and add more if necessary).

Strain stock through a sieve. Reserve stock and remove very small bones from meat.

Heat ghee and fry sliced onions till golden. Add ground onions, ginger, garlic, turmeric, red chilli and one tsp salt. Cook, adding curd a little at a time till masala is well browned and ghee separates.

Add cooked meat and brain, pour in enough stock to make a thick gravy, cover and cook on low heat for 15-20 minutes.

MASALA CHAAP
Masala Chops

Serves: 5-6

1 kg mutton chops
150 gm (1 large) onion, sliced
6-8 cloves garlic, ground
2 inch piece ginger, chopped
½ tsp each salt and turmeric powder
Pinch powdered red chilli
200 gm (4 medium) tomatoes, skinned and chopped
½ tsp garam masala powder
2 green chillies, chopped
2 tbsp chopped fresh coriander
2 tbsp ghee

Put chops in a large pan with garlic, salt, turmeric, red chilli and one third each of onion and ginger. Pour over 250 ml water and cook on medium heat for 40-50 minutes till tender, adding more water if necessary. Transfer chops to a greased baking dish. (Keep any left over cooking liquid aside for later use.) Sprinkle garam masala, green chillies, one third each of onions, ginger and tomato and half coriander over chops in pan. Bake in a moderate oven, 350°C (180°F) for 20 minutes.

Heat ghee and fry remaining onions golden. Add remaining ginger, tomatoes and coriander. Stir in reserved cooking liquid. Cook till thickened, pour over chops and serve.

KATHI KABAB
Boneless Mutton Kabab

Serves: 6-8

1 kg boneless mutton, cut in 1 inch cubes
8 dried kachri or 2 inch piece raw papaya
4 dried figs
4 medium onions
8 cloves garlic
1 inch piece ginger
2 inch piece raw papaya
12 black peppercorns
100 gm yellow mustard seeds
1 tsp cumin seeds
4 tbsp curd
4 tbsp ghee
Onion rings and lime wedges to garnish

Soak kachri and figs in water for 4 hours (It is not necessary to soak papaya if using). Drain and grind with onions, garlic, ginger and papaya. Roast separately, peppercorns, mustard seeds and cumin seeds on a griddle, grind very fine and stir into wet masala paste. Add curd and mix thoroughly. Marinate meat in this mixture and refrigerate overnight.

Thread pieces of meat onto skewers and cook under grill or on a barbecue, turning frequently till evenly browned. Cook for a further 10 minutes, basting with melted ghee and turning occasionally. Remove from skewers and transfer to a greased frying pan till ready to serve. Heat thoroughly and serve garnished with onion rings and lime wedges.

These can be served with drinks, or as part of the main meal.

KOFTA
Meatball Curry

Serves: 6-8

1 kg very finely minced mutton
1 large mutton bone
5 level tsp poppy seeds
300 gm (5 medium) onions
20 cloves garlic
1½ tsp salt
250 gm (1¼ cups) ghee
1 tsp turmeric powder
3 tsp powdered coriander seeds
1 tsp powdered red chilli
¾+½ tsp garam masala powder
4 medium tomatoes, skinned and chopped
2 inch piece ginger, finely chopped
7 heaped tsp roasted, ground and sieved parched gram (channa)
2 eggs
2 tbsp chopped fresh coriander leaves
6 green cardamoms
250 gm (2 cups) curd, whipped
Chopped fresh coriander to garnish

Soak poppy seeds in water for 30 minutes. Drain and grind very
fine. Mix thoroughly into mince, pounding it in. Keep aside.

Grind onions and garlic with salt. Heat ghee in a large pan and
fry onions and garlic over medium heat till golden. Add turmeric,
coriander powder, red chilli and ¾ tsp garam masala and cook,
stirring for 1-2 minutes adding 1-2 tsp water. Put bone into pan
and stir in tomatoes and ginger. Continue cooking till ghee
separates and masala is paste-like. Take 2 tbsp of masala and mix
into mince along with gram, eggs, fresh coriander and ½ tsp

garam masala. Beat thoroughly with your hand till mixture feels light and sticky. Using greased hands, form koftas of desired size. (One kg mince is usually enough for 20-25 koftas). Keep aside.

Add curd to masala in the pan, mix and add 750 ml water. Bring to boil and gently lower koftas into gravy. Reduce heat and cook uncovered for 10 minutes then cover and cook for 30-45 minutes more, shaking pan from time to time. Carefully lift and turn koftas with a slotted spoon. Shake pan and cook till they are a rich brown. Add green cardamom. Remove bone and sprinkle with chopped coriander before serving.

Serve with pulao for a typical Sunday lunch, or roti.

Note: Always use fresh mince. Koftas may break if frozen mince is used.

NARGISI KOFTA
Scotch Eggs - Mughlai Style

Serves: 8-10

Nargisi Kofta gets its name from the yellow and white of the egg which is said to resemble the Narcissus (Nargis). Nobody is quite sure whether the dish travelled from India to England to emerge as the Scotch Egg, or vice versa.

Kofta:

1 kg fine mince
3 medium onions, minced
1 pod garlic, peeled and ground
2 inch piece ginger, ground
1-2 green chillies, finely chopped
2 tsp salt
6 tbsp gram flour (besan)
2 eggs, lightly beaten
1 tsp garam masala powder
10 hardboiled eggs, shelled
500 gm (2½ cups) ghee for frying

Gravy:

150 gm (¾ cup) ghee
4-5 medium onions, minced
2½ inch piece ginger, ground
1 pod garlic, peeled and ground
3 tsp powdered coriander seeds
½ tsp turmeric powder
500 gm (6 large) tomatoes, skinned and chopped
250 gm (2 cups) curd, whipped
1 tsp garam masala powder
Chopped fresh coriander to garnish

Kofta: Cook mince with next 5 ingredients in one litre water for 30-45 minutes till dry. Cool and add gram flour, beaten eggs and garam masala. Beat thoroughly till mixture feels sticky. Divide into 10 parts. Shape each into a patty about 4 inches in diameter. Brush a hardboiled egg with water, place in the centre of patty and work mince around to enclose egg completely. Press firmly to seal any cracks.

Heat 500 gm ghee in a kadhai or deep frying pan and fry koftas till golden. Keep aside.

Gravy: Heat ghee in a large pan and fry minced onions till golden. Add 2 tsp water, ginger, garlic, coriander powder and turmeric. Stir and fry for 1-2 minutes. Add tomatoes and cook for 7-10 minutes still masala is paste-like. Stir in curd and cook for 5 minutes. Pour in one litre water and simmer for 15 minutes till gravy thickens. Remove from heat. Halve each kofta lengthwise and place in gravy with egg side up. Warm on low heat for 10 minutes. Serve carefully so that koftas do not break. An easier way is to pour gravy into an ovenproof dish, arrange koftas on top and heat in a low oven, 150°C (300°F) for 15-20 minutes. Serve garnished with chopped fresh coriander.

KEEMA MATAR
Mince with Green Peas

Serves: 6-8

Keema Matar along, with dry potatoes and poories, was a favourite for picnics and train journeys as it is dry and there is no danger of gravy spilling and making a mess.

In the days before corridor trains and restaurant cars a train journey required considerable planning. Bedrolls, the packing of which was an art, had to be unrolled at night and rolled up again before one's destination was reached. There was quite a flurry of activity early in the morning when the whole family travelled, as there was quite a lot of bedding to put away.

In the summer a tub with a large slab of ice was kept in the compartment under the fan. This functioned as an air-conditioner and also as a refrigerator as bottles of water, butter, mangoes and other perishables were put on the ice.

1 kg mince
2 tsp salt
1 tsp turmeric powder
Pinch powdered red chilli
20-25 cloves garlic, ground
2 inch piece ginger, ground
250 gm (2 cups) curd
250 gm (1¼ cups) ghee
250 gm (2 medium) onions, sliced
1 kg shelled green peas
1 tsp garam masala powder
2 tbsp fresh coriander
1-2 green chillies, chopped

Mix salt, turmeric, red chilli, garlic, ginger and curd with mince. Leave for one hour.

Heat ghee in a pan and fry onions till golden, drain and keep aside. Put mince into pan and cook stirring till liquid dries. Crumble onions into mince, stir and cook till well browned. Pour in one litre water, cover and cook for 30 minutes. Add peas and cook till tender and mince is dry. Stir in coriander, garam masala and green chillies.

Serve with roti, poori or parantha.

Variation:

Keema Gobi: This can be made in the same way. Add small florets of cauliflower for just 10 minutes before the end of cooking time so that they do not become mushy.

SHAMI KABAB
Fried Mince Kabab

Makes: 30-35

Kabab:

1 kg minced mutton
100 gm (½ cup) Bengal gram (chana dal)
12-15 cloves garlic
2 inch piece ginger, chopped
6 cloves
2 inch piece cinnamon
Seeds of 6-8 green cardamoms
2 bay leaves
2 tsp salt
2 eggs, lightly beaten
250 gm (1¼ cups) ghee for frying

Filling:

2-3 green chillies, chopped
3 inch piece ginger, chopped fine
4 tbsp chopped fresh coriander leaves
25 gm (approx. 20) almonds blanched and chopped

Garnish:

Onion rings
Lime wedges
Mint sprigs

Cook mince with next eight ingredients in 500 ml water for about 1-1½ hours till mince is tender and completely dry. Discard bay leaves and cinnamon and grind mixture to a fine paste. Mix in eggs.

Mix together all ingredients for filling. With greased hands take a little mince and form into a ball. Make a depression in the centre and put in a little filling. Pinch together to enclose filling and gently flatten with palms. Make all the kababs in the same way.

Fry in hot ghee in a frying pan till golden on both sides.

Garnish with onion rings, lime wedges and sprigs of mint.

KACHE KEEME KI TIKIA
Fried Mince Kabab

Makes: 30-35

A recipe from *Rezia ka Shahi Dastarkhwana*

Kabab:

1 kg finely minced mutton
1 inch piece raw papaya, ground
1 inch piece ginger, ground
2 tsp salt
100 gm (¾ cup) thick curd
2 tbsp ghee
2 medium onions, sliced
100 gm (1 cup) parched gram (channa), roasted, ground and sieved
3 level tbsp poppy seeds, roasted and ground
2 tsp chironji, roasted and ground
1½ tsp garam masala powder
1 inch piece cinnamon, ground
250 gm (1¼ cups) ghee for frying

Filling:

3 inch piece ginger, chopped fine
2-3 green chillies, chopped fine
4 tbsp chopped fresh coriander

Garnish:

Onion rings
Chopped fresh coriander

Mix papaya, ginger and salt with mince and leave to marinate for one hour. Tie curd in muslin and hang for one hour.

Heat 2 tbsp ghee and fry onions golden. Grind and mix remaining ingredients for kababs, except ghee, into mince.

Mix together all ingredients for filling. Using greased hands, take small amounts of mince and form into balls. Make depressions in the centre of each ball and put in a little filling. Pinch together to enclose filling and flatten with palms.

Put a little ghee on a griddle or a heavy based frying pan and heat on a slow fire. Place a few kababs on griddle, cover with domed lid and cook for 5 minutes on each side till golden. Drizzle a little ghee on griddle during the cooking process.

Serve garnished with onion rings and chopped fresh coriander.

BHUNVA KALEJI
Dry Liver

Serves: 6-8

Serve this liver with drinks or with fried eggs for breakfast.

1 kg mutton liver, cleaned and cut into 1 inch pieces
200 gm (3 medium) onions, sliced
8 cloves garlic, ground
1 inch piece ginger, ground
2 tsp poppy seeds, ground
1 tsp garam masala powder
½ tsp turmeric powder
4 medium tomatoes, skinned and chopped
1½ tsp salt
250 gm (2 cups) curd
100 gm (½ cup) ghee

Heat ghee in a pan and fry onions till golden. Remove onions from pan, drain, grind and keep aside.

Add garlic, ginger, poppy seeds, garam masala and turmeric into the same pan, stir and cook for 1-2 minutes. Add tomatoes and salt and cook till masala is paste-like. Add liver and ground, fried onions and cook on low heat for 15 minutes. Pour in curd and continue to cook till gravy is very thick and almost dry.

BHUNVA BHEJA
Curried Brain

Serves: 4-5

A recipe from Babu Shahi Bawarchi.

4 sheep's brains, membranes removed
1 tsp turmeric powder
1 litre water
200 gm (1 cup) ghee
250 gm (2 large) onions, sliced
10-12 cloves garlic, ground
1 inch piece ginger, ground
2 tsp coriander powder
Seeds of 6 green cardamoms, crushed
½ tsp cloves, ground
Pinch red chilli powder
1 tsp salt
250 gm (2 cups) curd
Chopped fresh coriander

Put brains in a pan with water and turmeric. Bring to boil and remove from heat. Drain brains and cut each into 6-8 pieces.

Heat ghee in a pan and fry onions golden. Remove onions and keep aside. In the same ghee put all the spices and salt. Cook, stirring in curd a little at a time. Crumble in fried onions, add 100 ml water and cook till gravy is very thick. Stir in brains and cook for 5-10 minutes, taking care that they do not disintegrate. Sprinkle with chopped fresh coriander and serve.

BHEJA METHI
Brain with Fenugreek

Serves: 4-5

A recipe from *Rezia ka Shahi Dastarkhwana*

4 sheep's brains, membranes removed
25 cloves garlic
2 tbsp mustard oil
4 tbsp ghee
½ tsp fenugreek seeds
1 inch piece ginger, ground
3 tsp powdered coriander seeds
½ tsp garam masala powder
100 gm (¾ cup) curd
2 tbsp fenugreek leaves, chopped
1 tsp salt

Tie garlic in a piece of muslin and crush. Squeeze out juice into 300 ml water. Reserve 4 tbsp of garlic water and wash brains with the rest. Rub brains with mustard oil and keep aside.

Heat ghee in a pan and fry fenugreek seeds till they crackle. Add ginger, coriander, garam masala and curd. Stir and cook for 1-2 minutes, adding reserved garlic water a little at a time. Put in brains, fenugreek leaves and salt and cook on low heat for 15-20 minutes. Break up brains while cooking, but do not mash them.

Chicken and Fish

These days it is an easy matter to buy chicken—one can walk into a shop and buy dressed chicken, frozen chicken or even specific cuts of chicken. But at one time they could only be bought live from the market and there was a special skill in choosing a good specimen. The *Ain-I-Akbari* tells us that '...fowls, ducks etc. are fattened by the cooks; fowls are never kept less than a month'.

Even when we were children, the cook brought live chicken home and we took a ghoulish delight in watching it being slaughtered.

For parties people made sure of getting their chicken well in advance; this was not without risk, as at one party when lunch was inordinately delayed, a distraught cook informed the hostess that the chicken had run away!

So, as Mrs Beeton would have said, 'First catch your chicken'.

Note: All recipes are for chicken with the skin removed.

CHAAR MAGAZ KA MURGH
Chicken with Melon Seeds

Serves: 4-5

This chicken is cooked with the seeds of marsh melon, watermelon, pumpkin and cucumber, which is known as chaar magaz. The finished dish has a white appearance and a delicate flavour.

1 whole chicken (approx. 1 kg)

Stuffing:

4 slices white bread, without crust
½ cup milk
2 tbsp ghee
1 medium onion, chopped
2 eggs, hardboiled and chopped
½ tsp salt

Masala:

50 gm (6 tbsp) poppy seeds
150 gm chaar magaz (melon, pumpkin and cucumber seeds)
50 gm (⅓ cup) almonds, blanched
Seeds of 8-10 green cardamoms
1 nutmeg
9 cloves
100 gm (½ cup) ghee
1-2 tsp salt
150 gm (1¼ cup) curd
Pinch saffron dissolved in hot water
2-3 drops kewra essence

Wash chicken and clean the inside.

Stuffing: Soak bread in milk. Heat 2 tbsp ghee in a pan and fry onion till just beginning to colour. Squeeze out bread and mix with onion, eggs and salt. Stuff chicken with this mixture.

Masala: Soak poppy seed and chaar magaz separately in water for 2-3 hours. Drain and grind with almonds, cardamom, nutmeg and cloves to a very fine paste. Keep aside.

Heat 100 gms ghee in a large pan and carefully fry chicken on all sides without allowing it to brown.

Add magaz paste, curd and salt. Cover and cook on low heat for 45 minutes to one hour till chicken is tender. Add saffron and kewra.

Joint chicken before serving if desired.

SANDALI MURGH
White Chicken Curry

Serves: 4-5

A recipe from Mrs Meera Narain.

1 chicken, jointed (approx. 1 kg)
100 gm (½ cup) ghee
750 ml milk
25 gm (3 tbsp) chaar magaz (melon, pumpkin and cucumber seeds)
4 heaped tsp poppy seeds
25 gm (approx. 20) almonds, blanched
2-3 blades mace
½ nutmeg
Seeds of 6 green cardamoms
1½ tsp salt

Heat ghee in a pan and lightly fry chicken. Remove and put into another pan with milk. Cook for 20-30 minutes till tender.

Soak magaz and poppy seeds separately in water for 2-3 hours. Drain and grind with almonds, mace nutmeg and cardamom seeds. Fry paste for 2-3 minutes in ghee left over from frying chicken. Add to cooked chicken along with salt. Cover and simmer on very low heat for 10-15 minutes.

KUNDAN MURGH
White Chicken

Serves: 4-5

A recipe from Babu Shahi.

1 chicken, jointed (appox 1 kg)
250 gm (2 cups) curd
5 green chillies
2 tbsp ghee
5 whole green cardamoms
2 bay leaves
250 ml milk
3 tbsp desiccated coconut
1½ tsp salt

Wash and dry chicken.

Whip curd and put into a pan with whole green chillies. Stir over moderate heat just till it comes to boil. Remove from heat and set aside.

Heat ghee in a pan and fry cardamoms and bay leaves for one minute. Add chicken and cook for 2-3 minutes—do not allow chicken to brown. Add milk and coconut and cook over moderate heat for 30 minutes.

Strain curd into chicken, discarding chillies. Add salt and cook for 10 minutes or till chicken is tender.

HARE MASALE KA MURGH
Chicken in Green Masala

Serves: 4-5

1 chicken, jointed (approx. 1 kg)
1 small onion
10 cloves garlic
1 inch piece ginger
1-2 green chillies, de-seeded
A good handful fresh coriander leaves
250 gm (2 cups) curd
1½ tsp salt
2 tbsp ghee

Wash and dry chicken. Grind together onion, garlic, ginger, green chillies and coriander. Mix in curd and salt, add chicken and marinate for one hour.

Heat ghee in a pan and add chicken with marinade. Cover and cook on a low heat, for 40-45 minutes till chicken is tender.

MURGH KORMA
Rich Chicken Curry

Serves: 4-5

1 chicken, jointed (approx. 1 kg)
200 gm (1 cup) ghee
200 gm (3 medium) onions, sliced
20 cloves garlic, ground
1 inch piece ginger, ground
2 tsp powdered coriander seeds
½ tsp turmeric powder
6 whole green cardamoms, roughly crushed
1 tsp garam masala powder
1 tsp salt
2 medium tomatoes, skinned and chopped
200 gm (1½ cups) curd
Chopped fresh coriander

Heat ghee in a pan and fry onions golden. Remove onions and keep aside.

Into the same ghee add garlic, ginger, coriander powder, turmeric, cardamom and garam masala. Stir and fry for 2-3 minutes, adding 2-4 tsp water. Stir in tomatoes and salt and cook till masala is paste-like.

Cook chicken joints in masala till well browned. Crumble in fried onions and add curd. Cover and cook on low heat stirring occasionally, for 30 minutes or till done. Sprinkle with chopped fresh coriander and serve.

MURGH MUSALLAM - 1
Whole Masala Chicken

Serves: 4-5

A recipe from Babu Shahi.

1 whole chicken (approx. 1 kg)

Stuffing:

2 eggs, hardboiled and chopped
25 gm (approx. 20) almonds, chopped
25 gm (2 tbsp) pistachios, chopped

Masala:

250 gm (1¼ cups) ghee
250 gm (2 large) onions, sliced
12 cloves garlic, ground
1 inch piece ginger, ground
2 tsp powdered coriander seeds
½ tsp powdered red chilli
10 cloves, ground
Seeds of 6-8 green cardamoms, ground
250 gm (2 cups) curd
1½ tsp salt

Mix together eggs and nuts, stuff chicken with these and stich up opening.

Heat ghee in a pan and fry onions till golden. Remove onions and keep aside. Add all spices into the same pan. Stir and cook for 5 minutes, adding curd a little at a time. Add salt.

Put chicken into masala, crumble in fried onions, cover and cook on low heat for 45 minutes to one hour till chicken is tender. Turn chicken once or twice during the cooking process.

MURGH MUSALLAM - 2
Whole Masala Chicken

Serves: 4-5

1 whole chicken (approx. 1 kg)
2 hard boiled eggs, chopped

Marinade:

25 gm (approx. 20) almonds, blanched
25 gm (3 tbsp) chironji
25 gm (3 tbsp) poppy seeds
25 gm (3 tbsp) desiccated coconut
Seeds of 6 green cardamoms
6 cloves
2 pieces cinnamon, 1 inch each
2 tsp coriander seeds, roasted
½ tsp cumin seeds, roasted
Pinch each of red chilli, turmeric and garam masala powders
1½ tsp salt
250 gm (2 cups) curd

Gravy:

250 gm (1¼ cups) ghee
250 gm (2 large) onions, finely sliced
2 green chillies, chopped
2 tbsp chopped fresh coriander

Clean chicken and prick all over with a fork.

Marinade: Grind all dry ingredients for marinade and mix with
curd. Coat chicken with this mixture and marinate for one hour.
   Stuff marinated chicken with egg and stitch up opening.

Gravy: Heat ghee in a pan and fry onions till golden. Stir in chillies and fresh coriander.

Put chicken with marinade into pan and cook for a few minutes on all sides. Pour over 300 ml water. Cover and cook for 30-45 minutes till tender. Turn the chicken once or twice during the cooking process.

Serve with parantha.

MURG MUSALLAM - 3
Whole Masala Chicken

Serves: 4-5

This recipe for whole masala chicken was given by my grandmother to my sister when she got married. I reproduce it in her words translated from Hindi (1 chatak is roughly 60 gm).

Chicken should be young
Take 1 chatak almonds and grind
Grind 1 chatak coriander seeds
Grind ½ chatak poppy seeds
Chillies as desired. For one chicken use 1½ large red Patna chillies
Salt as desired
4 annas worth garam masala (use 1 tsp)
Juice of 1 lime
Pinch mace flakes

Prick chicken all over with fork. Mix together all ingredients and coat chicken with masala. Leave for one hour.

Cook chicken in a little ghee on low heat till tender.

Take a pinch of saffron, grind with a few drops kewra essence and add to chicken. Put chicken on dum. This is for plain chicken.

For stuffed chicken make yakhni pulao and stuff chicken with this. Some ground almonds and some raisins should be added to pulao before stuffing.

For stuffing without rice, take some boiled potatoes and peas, chopped hardboiled eggs and a little khoya (dried unsweetened condensed milk). Mix together and stuff chicken before cooking.

SOOKHA MASALA MURGH
Dry Masala Chicken

Serves: 4-5

1 chicken, jointed (approx. 1 kg)
2 green chillies
1 tsp powdered red chilli
2 tsp powdered coriander seeds
½ tsp turmeric powder
½ tsp aniseed (saunf)
6-8 cloves garlic
5-6 black peppercorns
1 tsp salt
200 gm (1 cup) ghee

Clean and dry chicken pieces. Grind all ingredients except salt and ghee and rub over chicken. Leave to marinate for 1-2 hours.

In a pan take 200 ml water and one tsp salt. Put in marinated chicken, bring to boil then simmer for 15-20 minutes till dry and chicken is just tender—do not overcook.

Heat ghee and fry chicken over low heat for 10 minutes till golden. Serve immediately.

Very good served with drinks.

MACHCHI KORMA
Fish Curry

Serves: 5-6

1 kg fish, boned and cut in pieces
1½ tsp cumin seeds
2 tbsp coriander seeds
2 tbsp poppy seeds
2 tbsp sesame seeds
2 tbsp chironji
100 gm (½ cup) ghee
100 gm (2 small) onions, sliced
10-12 cloves garlic, ground
1 inch piece ginger, ground
½ tsp turmeric powder
1½ tsp salt
200 gm (1⅔ cups) curd
2 tbsp chopped fresh coriander for garnish

Wash fish.

Roast separately cumin, coriander, poppy, sesame and chironji. Grind and keep aside.

Heat ghee in a pan and fry onions golden. Remove onions with a slotted spoon and keep aside.

Into the same pan add garlic, ginger, turmeric and salt. Stir and cook for one minute. Remove from heat, add ground spices and whipped curd. Crumble in fried onions and mix thoroughly. Add fish pieces, return to low heat and simmer for 10-15 minutes till fish is cooked.

Sprinkle with fresh coriander and serve with rice or roti.

MACHCHI KE KOFTE
Fish Kofta

Serves: 6-8

1 kg fish with bone, sliced
2 bay leaves
5-6 cloves
½ tsp black peppercorn
1 inch piece cinnamon
5 green cardamoms
1½ tsp salt
250-300 gm (1½ cups) ghee
3 large onions, finely chopped
2 eggs
4 level tbsp flour
1 tbsp chopped fresh coriander
2 inch piece ginger, ground
1 tsp mustard seeds
6 cloves garlic, ground
1 tbsp cumin seeds
2 tbsp coriander seeds
2 tbsp poppy seeds
1 tbsp chironji
150 gm (1¼ cups) curd
1 tsp turmeric powder
Chopped fresh coriander to garnish

Put fish in a large pan with bay leaves, cloves, peppercorns, cinnamon, cardamom and salt. Pour over 500 ml water, bring to boil, reduce heat, cover and simmer for 15 minutes till fish flakes. Drain fish and reserve liquid. Discard spices, carefully remove skin and bones and discard. Mash fish.

Heat one tbsp ghee in a pan and fry one third chopped onions till pale gold. Mix into mashed fish along with eggs, flour, fresh coriander and 1 tsp ground ginger.

With oiled hands shape fish mixture into walnut size balls and deep fry in hot ghee till golden. Keep aside.

Heat 4 tbsp ghee and fry remaining onions till golden. Add mustard seeds, then stir in garlic and remaining ginger. Cook, stirring for 1-2 minutes, adding 2-4 tsp of water. Remove from heat.

Roast separately cumin, coriander, poppy and chironji. Grind and add to onion mixture. Stir in whipped curd and turmeric, return to heat and cook, stirring continuously, till ghee separates.

Pour in reserved fish stock and cook for 10 minutes. Gently add koftas to pan and simmer on low heat for 20-30 minutes. Garnish with fresh coriander and serve with rice.

MASALA POMFRET
Whole Stuffed Pomfret

Serves: 4-5

1 whole pomfret (approx. 500 gm)
4 whole, dried red chillies, seeded
1 tbsp malt vinegar
1½ tsp cumin seeds
10-12 cloves garlic
1 inch piece ginger
1 tsp salt
1 tsp sugar
100 gm (½ cup) ghee

Remove fins of fish. (The head and tail may be cut off or left, as desired). Slit from one side, clean the inside, wash and leave to dry.

Soak chillies in vinegar for 15 minutes, grind along with cumin, garlic and ginger. Mix in salt and sugar. Put this paste inside fish and leave for at least 2 hours.

Heat ghee in a large frying pan and fry fish on low heat for 5-10 minutes on each side.

Chicken and Fish

SOOKHE MASALE KI MACHCHI
Masala Fried Fish

Serves: 4-5

1 kg boneless fish, cut into 2 inch pieces
12-15 cloves garlic
2 inch piece ginger
2 tsp powdered coriander seeds
1 tsp salt
Pinch powdered red chilli
Juice of ½ lime
2 cups breadcrumbs
250 gm (1¼ cups) ghee
Lime wedges to garnish

Clean and dry fish.

Grind garlic and ginger and combine with coriander, salt, chilli and lime juice. Rub over fish and leave to marinate for 1-2 hours.

Spread breadcrumbs on a plate and coat fish pieces, pressing crumbs in to hold masala in place. Heat ghee in a frying pan and fry fish till golden on all sides.

Garnish with lime wedges and serve.

Ideal to serve with drinks.

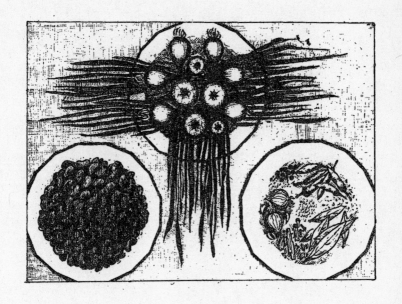

Lentils

D al is an extremely versatile ingredient and is used all over the country in a number of ways. Soaked and ground dal can be made into many different dishes.

Among Mathurs Banias and Khatris the wedding preparations traditionally begin with the making of mangories. These are small dried lentil pyramids used in a variety of ways.

A large quantity of washed husked green bean (mung) paste is prepared and the ladies of the family sit and make the mangories, swaying back and forth and singing quite tunelessly as they do so.

To make or (to use the literal translation of the Hindi word) to 'break' mangories, you take some mung dal paste in your hand and using the thumb and index finger, you drop small amounts of paste onto a straw mat—thus 'breaking' each one. These are left to dry in the sun for 2-3 days and then stored and cooked as needed. Now of course mangories are available in packets at most grocers.

SOOKHI MANGORI
Dried Mangori

Serves: 6-8

Mangori:

> 250 gm (¼ cup) husked green beans (dhuli mung ki dal)
> ½ inch piece ginger
> Pinch asafoetida
> 4 tbsp ghee

Gravy:

> 2 tbsp ghee
> 2 medium onions, grated
> 6 cloves garlic, ground
> 1 inch piece ginger, ground
> 2 tsp powdered coriander seeds
> 1 tsp turmeric powder
> 1 tsp salt
> Pinch powdered red chilli
> 2 tomatoes, skinned and chopped
> ½ tsp garam masala powder

Mangori: Wash dal and soak in cold water for 8-10 hours. Drain and grind along with ginger and asafoetida to a fine paste. Beat well.

Take a small amount of paste in your hand and using first two fingers and thumb, drop a small amount of paste onto a straw mat. Proceed till all the paste is used up. Place mangories in sun for 2-3 days till dry. (You can use 250 gm of the packaged mangories).

Heat 4 tbsp ghee and lightly fry dried mangories. Keep aside.

Gravy: Heat 2 tbsp ghee and fry onions till golden. Stir in 3-4 tsp water, add garlic and ginger and cook for one minute. Stir in coriander, turmeric, salt, chilli and tomatoes. Cook for 5-7 minutes till mixture is paste-like. Add mangori and cook for 1-2 minutes.

Pour in one litre water, cover and cook on low heat for 15-20 minutes till mangories are tender.

TALI MANGORI
Fried Mangori

Serves: 6-8

A recipe from Mrs Manju Vira.

> 200 gm (1 cup) husked green beans (dhuli mung ki dal)
> 250 ml mustard oil
> Ginger tomato gravy (see recipe on pg. 120)
> 2 tbsp chopped fresh coriander

Wash dal and soak in water for 8-10 hours. Drain and grind to a very fine paste. Beat well with your hand.

Heat oil in a flat kadhai or frying pan till smoking. Take a handful of paste and, using thumb and index finger, 'break' mangories into oil. Reduce heat and cook without turning till bubbles appear on the surface. This allows the steam to escape and ensures that the mangories do not become hard.

Turn and cook till golden.

Put into ginger tomato gravy and cook for 10-15 minutes, adding water if necessary. Sprinkle with chopped fresh coriander and serve.

DAL KI PAKORI
Green Bean Fritters in Gravy

Serves: 5-6

200 gm (1 cup) husked green beans (dhuli mung ki dal)
¼ tsp baking soda
250 gm (1¼ cups) + 3 tbsp ghee
2 medium onions
5-6 cloves garlic, ground
1 inch piece ginger, ground
1½ tsp powdered coriander seeds
1 tsp turmeric powder
1 tsp salt
Pinch powdered red chilli
1 medium tomato, skinned and chopped
½ tsp garam masala powder
Chopped fresh coriander for garnish

Wash dal and soak in water overnight.

Next day stir baking soda into pre-soaked dal, and leave for half an hour.

Drain and grind dal to a fine paste. Beat with your hand till paste is fluffy and holds its shape.

Heat 250 gms ghee in a kadhai or deep frying pan till smoking. (To test if ghee is hot enough, drop a little paste into kadhai. It should rise to the surface almost immediately).

Using moistened fingers drop small amounts of paste into ghee. When bubbles appear on the surface, turn and fry till pale gold. Drain and keep aside.

Chop one onion and grind the other. Heat 3 tbsp ghee and fry chopped onion golden. Stir in ground onion, garlic and ginger and cook for 1-2 minutes, adding 2-3 tsp water. Stir in coriander powder, turmeric, salt, chilli and tomato. Cover and cook on low heat for 5-7 minutes till masala is thick and paste-like. Pour in one litre water and add pakories and garam masala. Cover and cook for 10 minutes. The gravy should be quite thin.

Sprinkle with chopped fresh coriander and serve.

DAL KI KALEJI
Green Bean Cubes in Gravy

Serves: 6-8

There is an old tradition amongst Mathurs of making vegetarian items look like meat. For dal ki kaleji, husked green beans are soaked and ground to a paste. This is boiled, cut into cubes, fried and cooked in gravy to resemble liver. It is a pleasant vegetarian dish though it does not taste in the least bit like liver!

Kaleji:

200 gm (1 cup) husked green beans (dhuli mung ki dal)
2 medium onions, quartered
2 green chillies, de-seeded and finely chopped
½ inch piece ginger, finely chopped
2 tsp chopped fresh coriander
½ tsp salt
¼ tsp baking soda

250 gm (1¼ cups) ghee for frying

Gravy:

100 gm (½ cup) ghee
4 medium onions, ground
10 cloves garlic, ground
1 inch piece ginger, ground
3 tsp powdered coriander seeds
½ tsp turmeric powder
2-3 tomatoes, skinned and chopped
4 tbsp curd
1 tsp salt
½ tsp garam masala powder
1 tbsp chopped fresh coriander

Kaleji: Wash dal and soak for 8-10 hours in water. Drain and grind to a fine paste along with onions. Mix in remaining ingredients and beat thoroughly. Put into a clean piece of muslin or a napkin, and tie securely.

Have ready a large pan of boiling water and put in tied up dal. Boil for one minute, then reduce heat and simmer for 45 minutes. Lift out and cool slightly. Unwrap cooked dal and cut into ½-¾ inch cubes.

Heat 250 gms ghee in a kadhai or deep frying pan and fry cubes till golden. Drain and keep aside.

Gravy: Heat 100 gms ghee and fry ground onions golden. Add garlic and ginger and fry for 1-2 minutes, adding 1-2 tsp water. Stir in coriander powder, turmeric and tomatoes and cook for 5-7 minutes till mixture is paste-like. Add whipped curd, salt, garam masala and fresh coriander, pour in 500 ml water and simmer for 5 minutes. Put in pieces of fried dal, cover and cook on low heat for 10 minutes.

DAL KA KEEMA
Husked Green Beans with Green Peas

Serves: 6-8

A recipe from Mrs Shamsher Bahadur.

125 gm (⅔ cup) husked green beans (dhuli mung ki dal)
250 gm (1¼ cups) + 100 gm (½ cup) ghee
4 medium onions, ground
20 cloves garlic, ground
1 inch piece ginger, ground
3 tsp powdered coriander seeds
½ tsp turmeric powder
3 medium tomatoes, skinned and chopped
1 tsp salt
½ tsp garam masala powder
6 tbsp curd
250 gm shelled green peas
2 tbsp chopped fresh coriander

Wash dal and soak in water for 8-10 hours. Drain and grind coarsely.

Heat 250 gms ghee in a frying pan and fry dal till golden. Keep scraping pan to prevent dal from sticking, and do not allow it to become too dark. Drain and keep aside.

Heat 100 gms ghee and fry ground onion golden. Add garlic, ginger and a little water and cook for 1-2 minutes. Stir in coriander powder, turmeric, tomatoes and salt and cook till mixture is paste-like. Add fried dal, pour in 500 ml water, cover and cook on low heat for 10-15 minutes. Add peas and cook for a further 15-20 minutes till peas are tender, adding more water if necessary.

Stir in garam masala and curd and cook, stirring, till mixture is dry.

Sprinkle with chopped coriander and serve with roti, poori or parantha.

AALAN KA SAAG
Split Green Beans with Spinach

Serves: 6-8

150 gm (¾ cup) split green beans (chhilke ki mung ki dal)
1 tsp salt
1 tsp turmeric powder
2 handfuls spinach leaves, roughly chopped
4 tbsp gram flour (besan)
1 tbsp ghee
Pinch asafoetida
½ tsp cumin seeds
2-3 dried whole red chillies
2 tsp pure ghee

Wash dal and put into a pan with 1½ litres water. Bring to boil, skim off foam that rises to the surface, reduce heat, add salt and turmeric and cook for 35-40 minutes till tender. (You may need to add extra water). Stir and mash dal against sides of pan. Add spinach and cook for 5 minutes.

Mix gram flour with 250 ml water and pour into dal. Stir and cook on low heat till thick.

Heat one tbsp ghee and fry asafoetida, cumin and red chillies and pour into dal. Stir in 2 tsp pure ghee and serve with crisp phulka.

SOOKHI URAD KI DAL
Dry Black Beans

Serves: 4-5

125 gm (⅔ cup) husked black beans (dhuli urad ki dal)
2 tsp pure ghee
1 tsp chopped ginger
1 green chilli, chopped
1 tsp salt
½ tsp turmeric powder
Pinch asafoetida
½ tsp cumin seeds
1-2 dried whole red chillies

Wash dal and soak in water for one hour. Drain.

Heat one tsp ghee in a pan and fry ginger and green chilli for one minute. Add drained dal, salt, turmeric and enough water to cover, plus ½ cup more. Bring to boil, reduce heat and cook uncovered without stirring for 20-25 minutes till water is absorbed and dal is tender; each grain of dal should be visible.

Just before serving, heat one tsp ghee and fry asafoetida, cumin and red chillies. Pour over dal and gently stir to heat through.

MUNG DAL AUR PALAK
Green Beans with Spinach

Serves: 6-8

200 gm (1 cup) split or husked green beans (dhuli mung ki dal)
250 gm spinach
4 tbsp oil
1 tsp chopped ginger
1-2 green chillies, chopped
Pinch asafoetida
½ tsp cumin seeds
1 tsp salt
½ tsp turmeric
Juice of ½ a lime

Wash dal. Wash and finely chop spinach.

Heat oil in a pan and fry ginger, green chillies, asafoetida and cumin for one minute. Add dal and spinach and cook for another 1-2 minutes. Add salt, turmeric and 1½ litres water. Cook, uncovered on low heat, stirring from time to time till dal is tender. (You may need to add extra water). Stir in lime juice and serve.

MANDHIYA
Pigeon Peas in Rice Konji

Serves: 4-5

This Bania dish uses the water left over from boiling rice which, instead of being thrown away, is mixed with dal and spices to make a tasty accompaniment for the rice.

500 ml water drained from boiled rice
150 ml cooked, husked pigeon peas (arhar dal)
300 gm (2½ cups) curd
½ tsp each turmeric, ground ginger, ground kachri, ground dried green mango (amchur)
Pinch powdered red chilli
2 green chillies, cut into 4 pieces each
1 tsp salt
1 tbsp ghee
2 cloves
½ tsp cumin seeds
Pinch asafoetida

Mix dal, curd, ground spices, red and green chillies and salt with rice water.

Heat ghee and fry cloves, cumin and asafoetida. Stir into mixture and cook for 5-10 minutes.

The consistency should remain quite thin.

Serve with rice.

TAKKE PAISE
Gram Flour Pennies

Serves: 6-8

The story goes that when Aurangzeb imprisoned his father, Shahjehan, he asked the latter to choose any one item of food and that would be the only thing served to him for a whole year. Shahjehan is said to have chosen the humble chana because there is such a variety of ways in which it can be cooked.

This recipe and the following are made from chana in its form of gram flour.

Takke paise:

1 onion, roughly chopped
4 dried kachri, soaked for 2 hours
2 dried figs, soaked for 2 hours
10 cloves garlic
1½ tsp salt
1 tsp garam masala powder
500 gm gram flour (besan)
100 gm (½ cup) ghee + 250 gm (1¼ cups) for frying

Gravy:

150 gm (¾ cup) ghee
250 gm (2 large) onions, ground
20 cloves garlic, ground
1 inch piece ginger, chopped fine
½ tsp powdered red chilli
1½ tsp turmeric powder
½ tsp garam masala powder
2 tsp powdered coriander seeds
1 tsp salt

4 medium tomatoes, skinned and chopped
200 gm (1⅓ cups) curd
Chopped fresh coriander to garnish

Takke paise: Grind together onions, kachri, figs and garlic. Mix into gram flour with salt and garam masala. Rub in 100 gms ghee. Gradually add enough water (approx. ½ cup) to make a stiff dough. Divide dough into 3-4 parts and roll each into a sausage shape one inch in diameter. Bring a large pan of water to boil, drop in rolls of gram flour and cook for 30 minutes. Drain and cool.

Cut cooked dough into thin slices and fry in 250 gms ghee till pale gold.

Gravy: Heat ghee and fry onions golden. Add garlic, ginger and remaining spices. Stir and cook for 2-3 minutes, adding 1-2 tsp water. Add salt and tomatoes and cook till ghee separates, then pour in whipped curd and 4 cups water.

Bring gravy to the boil and put in fried pieces of dough. Cook for 1-2 minutes, reduce heat, cover and cook for 10-15 minutes.

Serve garnished with chopped fresh coriander.

KADHI

Gram Flour Curry with Dumplings

Serves: 6-8

There are many different ways of making kadhi all over India.
This is the recipe always used in our family.

250 gm (2 cups) gram flour (besan)
250 gm (2 cups) sour curd
2 tbsp + 250 gm (1¼ cups) ghee
¼ tsp asafoetida
½ tsp cumin seeds
½ tsp fenugreek seeds
3-4 dried whole red chillies
1½ tsp salt
1 tsp turmeric powder

Kadhi: Sieve gram flour. Put half into a large bowl. Whip curd,
add to gram flour and mix well. Stir in 1½ litres water to make a
thin mixture.

In a large pan heat 2 tbsp ghee. Stir in asafoetida, cumin,
fenugreek and red chillies. Do not allow chillies to turn black.
Quickly pour in gram flour mixture. Add salt and turmeric and
cook over medium heat stirring constantly till mixture bubbles
and thickens. Keep aside.

Pakoris: To the remaining gram flour add enough water to make a
soft paste. Beat thoroughly. Drop a small amount of paste into a
bowl of water—it should rise to the surface, if not, beat more till
mixture is light enough.

(You can cheat and add ¼ tsp baking powder, specially if the weather is humid.)

Heat 250 gms ghee till smoking, drop spoonfuls of paste into hot ghee and fry golden. Put into kadhi mixture and cook for 10-15 minutes.

Serve with plain boiled rice and south ki chutney.

Vegetables

Many of the vegetables we use everyday were fairly late entrants to India.

Potatoes, without which most meals are incomplete today, were native to South America. The Dutch began to cultivate them in South Africa and the British got seed-potatoes from them and introduced them to India. They were first grown in Bengal and were cultivated extensively in North India only as late as 1830. Initially only the Europeans ate potatoes. Later they were accepted by the Muslims and then were used widely throughout the country.

We cannot imagine life without tomatoes and chillies, both of which originated in Mexico or Peru and were brought to India by the Europeans. Tomatoes reached India via Europe in 1850. The colonials also brought cauliflower, beans and peas.

The only vegetable recipe in the *Ain-I-Akbari* is for (leafy greens) saag, although the lists of prices mention onions, garlic, turnips, carrots, bitter gourd, pumpkin, parwal, courgettes, kachalu, yam and various greens such as bathua and chaulai.

SAAG
Masala Spinach

Serves: 4-5

The recipe for Saag from the *Ain-I-Akbari* says 'It is made of spinach and other greens, and is one of the most pleasant dishes. 10s. spinach, fennel etc., 1½s. ghi, 1s. onions, ½ s. fresh ginger, 5½ m.of pepper, ½ m. cardamom and cloves; this gives six dishes'.

The use of 'fennel' in this recipe could be the translator's error as I have not been able to trace any recipe using fennel greens. I have used dill (sua bhaji) instead.

Reducing this recipe to one tenth, (where s stands for seer or one kg and m for misqual which is the weight of 96 grains of barley!) one gets the following:

> 1 kg spinach
> Handful of dill leaves (sua bhaji)
> 150 gm (¾ cup) ghee
> 100 gm (2 small) onions, finely chopped
> 2 inch piece ginger, ground
> ½ tsp salt
> ¼ tsp pepper
> 2 green cardamoms crushed
> 3-4 cloves, crushed

Pick only the leaves of the spinach. Wash spinach and dill thoroughly and chop fine.

Heat ghee in a pan and fry chopped onions till translucent. Stir in ginger, chopped greens, salt, pepper, cardamoms and cloves. Stir and cook uncovered for 7-10 minutes till tender.

SABUT CHHOTE ALU
Whole Small Potatoes

Serves: 6

½ kg small potatoes
2 tbsp ghee
1 tsp cumin seeds
½ tsp turmeric powder
1 tsp powdered coriander seeds
1 tsp powdered aniseed (saunf)
2 tsp powdered dried green mango (amchur)
½ tsp garam masala powder
1½ tsp salt

Choose really small, even sized potatoes. Wash thoroughly but do not peel. Discard any green ones.

Heat ghee in a kadhai or wok. Stir in cumin seeds and fry for one minute. Add potatoes, cook and stir for 1-2 minutes. Add remaining ingredients and stir to coat potatoes in the masala. Cover and cook over low heat, stirring occasionally. (If potatoes stick to bottom of pan, add 1-2 tbsp water). Test potatoes after 20 minutes to see if they are cooked through. Cover and cook for few minutes more till tender and completely dry.

SABUT BAINGAN
Whole Aubergines in Dry Masala

Serves: 6

½ kg small aubergines
1 tsp salt
½ tsp turmeric powder
1 tsp powdered aniseed (saunf)
1 tsp powdered coriander seeds
½ tsp garam masala powder
2 tbsp ghee

Wash and dry aubergines, leaving on the stems. Slit across twice almost to the stalk end.

Mix all dry ingredients together and rub a little inside each aubergine.

Heat ghee in a kadhai or frying pan and fry aubergines for 1-2 minutes, reduce heat, cover and cook for 15-20 minutes till tender, turning occasionally.

MASALA BAINGAN
Whole Aubergines with Thick Gravy

Serves: 6

½ kg small aubergines
2 tbsp ghee
2 medium onions, sliced
1 inch piece ginger, ground
10 cloves garlic, ground
2 tsp powdered coriander seeds
1 tsp turmeric powder
½ tsp garam masala powder
1 tsp salt
250 gm (3 large) tomatoes, skinned and chopped
Chopped fresh coriander

Wash and dry aubergines keeping them whole.

Heat ghee in a pan and fry onions pale gold. Add ginger and garlic, stir and cook for 1-2 minutes, adding a little water during the process. Stir in coriander powder, turmeric, garam masala, salt and tomatoes. Reduce heat, cover and cook for 5-10 minutes till mixture is paste-like. Put in aubergines, cover and cook for 30 minutes, turning occasionally, till done.

Sprinkle with fresh coriander and serve.

BAINGAN KA BHARTA
Mashed Aubergines in Curd

Serves: 4-5

1 large round aubergine (approx. 500 gm)
2 tbsp ghee
1 medium onion, finely chopped
1 inch piece ginger, finely chopped
2-3 green chillies, finely chopped
2 tbsp chopped fresh coriander
1 tsp salt
250 gm (2 cups) curd

Roast aubergine on a flame till skin is completely black. Cool and peel. (You could also cook the aubergine in boiling water for 10-15 minutes).

Mash aubergine and keep aside.

Heat ghee in a pan and fry onion till lightly coloured. Add mashed aubergine and cook for 5-10 minutes. Cool. Stir in ginger, chillies, coriander, salt and curd.

Chill and serve.

DOODH MATAR
Green Peas Cooked in Milk

Serves: 4-5

250 gm (2½ cups) shelled green peas
2 tbsp ghee
Pinch asafoetida
½ tsp cumin seeds
½ tsp turmeric powder
2 tsp powdered coriander seeds
¼ tsp powdered red chilli
200 ml milk
1 tsp salt

Heat ghee in a pan. Add asafoetida, cumin, turmeric, coriander and chilli and cook for 1-2 minutes.

Stir in peas, reduce heat, cover and cook for 10-15 minutes. Cool slightly and add milk. Cook on very low heat for further 10 minutes till peas are tender.

Put into a dish and stir in salt just before serving.

ADRAK TAMATAR GRAVY
Ginger Tomato Gravy

Serves: 6-8

This is a versatile gravy which can be used for potatoes, colocasia (arvi) and vegetable kofta.

200 ml mustard oil
2 inch piece ginger, chopped
2-3 green chillies, chopped
Pinch asafoetida
1 tsp cumin seeds
½ kg (3 large) tomatoes, skinned and pureed
1 tsp salt
½ tsp turmeric powder
2 tsp powdered coriander seeds
Pinch powdered red chilli

Heat oil in a pan and fry ginger till pink. Stir in green chillies, asafoetida and cumin and fry for 1-2 minutes.

Stir in remaining ingredients and cook on low heat till oil separates. Pour in 250 ml water and simmer for a few minutes.

Variations:
Alu aur Adrak Tamatar: Cook medium sized potatoes in boiling water for 20 minutes. Peel and prick all over with fork.

Fry in a little oil till pink, put into ginger tomato gravy and cook over low heat for 10-15 minutes till tender.

Arvi aur Adrak Tamatar: Peel and cut colocasia into small chunks. Fry till golden, put into ginger tomato gravy and cook on low heat for 5 minutes.

Tali Mangori: See recipe.

KARARI ARVI
Fried Colocasia

Serves: 4-5

My father-in-law had a cook who took pride in making fried arvi, which resembled fillet of fried fish. A vegetarian guest once mistakenly took fish, and swears to this day that he has never had such delicious arvi!

250 gm colocasia (arvi)
200 gm (1 cup) + 1 tbsp ghee
Pinch asafoetida
½ tsp thyme seeds (ajwain)
½ tsp powdered red chilli
1 tsp salt

Boil arvi till tender. Peel and cut in half lengthwise and flatten with palms.

Heat 200 gms ghee in a frying pan and fry arvi till crisp and golden. Drain and put into another pan.

Heat one tbsp ghee and fry asafoetida and thyme for one minute. Remove from heat, stir in chilli and salt. Pour over arvi. Cover and cook on very low heat for 5 minutes.

MASALA ARVI
Colocasia in Masala

Serves: 5-6

½ kg colocasia (arvi)
2 tbsp ghee
2 inch piece ginger, finely chopped
2-3 green chillies, chopped
Pinch asafoetida
¼ tsp thyme seed (ajwain)
½ tsp salt
½ tsp turmeric powder
1 tsp powdered coriander seeds
2 tbsp curd
2 tbsp chopped fresh coriander

Scrape arvi and cut into chunks.

Heat ghee in a pan and fry ginger for 2-3 minutes. Add chillies, asafoetida and thyme, Stir and fry for another minute. Put in arvi along with salt, turmeric and coriander powder. Pour in 250 ml water and cook till water is absorbed and arvi is tender. Remove from heat and add whipped curd and fresh coriander.

KELE KE PARSINDE
Green Banana Curry

Serves: 6-8

6 green cooking bananas
250 gm (1¼ cups) ghee for frying

Gravy:

100 gm (½ cup) ghee
3 medium onions, grated
8 cloves garlic, ground
1 inch piece ginger, ground
1 inch piece cinnamon
6 green cardamoms
Seeds of 3 black cardamoms, powdered
2 bay leaves
3 tsp powdered coriander seeds
1 tsp garam masala powder
1 tsp salt
250 gm (2 cups) curd
2 tbsp chopped fresh coriander

Bring a large pan of water to the boil, put in whole, unpeeled bananas and cook for 10 minutes. Drain, cool slightly and peel.

Cut each banana in half and then cut each piece lengthwise into half again. Keeping cut side down, use back of a fork and gently press to flatten bananas to ¼ inch thickness.

Heat 250 gms ghee in a kadhai or deep frying pan and fry bananas till golden. Drain and keep aside.

Gravy: Heat 100 gms ghee in a pan and fry grated onions on a moderate fire till golden. Add 2 tbsp water and stir for one minute. Add garlic and ginger and cook for 1-2 minutes. Stir in remaining spices and salt and cook for 2-3 minutes, adding curd a little at a time. Pour in 350 ml water, cover and cook on low heat for 10 minutes till gravy has thickened. Put fried bananas in gravy, cover and simmer for 5 minutes.

Sprinkle with chopped fresh coriander and serve.

LAGE LIPTE ALU
Potatoes in Thick Gravy

Serves: 4-5

½ kg (4 medium) potatoes
50 gm (3½ tbsp) ghee or mustard oil
1 inch piece ginger, finely chopped
2 green chillies, chopped
Pinch asafoetida
2-3 tomatoes, skinned and pureed (do not use packaged tomato puree)
½ tsp turmeric powder
2 tsp powdered coriander seeds
Pinch powdered red chilli
1 tsp salt
1 tbsp curd
Chopped fresh coriander

Wash potatoes and cook in boiling water till tender. Peel and cut into chunks. Break about one third of the potatoes with your hands.

Heat ghee in a pan and add next seven ingredients in the order given. Add all the potatoes and 250 ml water. Stir and cook for 5-10 minutes. Remove from heat and stir in curd. The gravy should be quite thick with the broken potatoes. Sprinkle chopped fresh coriander and serve with poories and saunf ki chutney.

DUM ALU
Fried Potato Curry

Serves: 6-8

1 kg medium sized potatoes
250 gm (1¼ cups) ghee for frying

Gravy:

200 gm (3 medium) onions
200 gm (1 cup) ghee
10 cloves garlic, ground
2 inch piece ginger, ground
½ tsp turmeric powder
½ tsp powdered red chilli
½ tsp powdered black pepper
1 tsp cumin seeds, roasted and ground
4 tsp coriander seeds, roasted and ground
2 tsp poppy seeds, roasted and ground
8 cloves, powdered
Seeds of 3 black cardamoms, powdered
Pinch powdered mace
2 pieces cinnamon, 1 inch each
6 green cardamoms
2-3 bay leaves
2 tsp salt
250 gm (2 cups) curd
2 tbsp chopped fresh coriander

Peel potatoes and cut each into half. Prick all over with a fork and soak in cold water for 15 minutes.

Drain and dry potatoes. Heat 250 gms ghee in a kadhai or deep frying pan and fry potatoes on moderate heat till golden on all sides. (You may need extra ghee). Keep aside.

Gravy: Finely slice half the onions and grind the other half.

Heat 200 gms ghee in a pan and fry sliced onions till golden. Add 2 tbsp water, stir in ground onions and cook for 2-3 minutes. Add garlic, ginger, all the spices and salt. Stir and cook on a low heat, adding curd a little at a time.

Put fried potatoes into masala and cook for 5 minutes. Pour in 250 ml water, cover and cook, stirring occasionally, for 20-30 minutes till potatoes are tender.

Garnish with chopped fresh coriander before serving.

SABUT BHINDI
Whole Okra

Serves: 5-6

500 gm tender, small okras
2 tsp powdered coriander seeds
1 tsp powdered aniseed (saunf)
½ tsp turmeric powder
1 tsp salt
Pinch powdered red chilli
100 ml mustard oil
Pinch asafoetida
½ tsp thyme seeds (ajwain)

Wash okras and dry thoroughly. Cut off stems and make a slit along length of okras.

Mix together powdered spices, salt and chilli. Put a little inside each okra pod.

Heat oil in a kadhai or frying pan, fry asafoetida and thyme for 1-2 minutes, put in okras and stir for one minute. Reduce heat, cover and cook for 20-30 minutes till okras are tender and completely dry.

GWAR KI PHALI
Cluster Beans

Serves: 4

250 gm cluster beans (gwar phalli)
200 ml mustard oil
Pinch asafoetida
½ tsp thyme seed (ajwain)
1 tsp chopped ginger
1 tsp powdered dried green mango (amchur)
½ tsp salt
Pinch powdered red chilli

Cook beans in boiling water till tender-crisp. Drain, cool and de-vein.

Heat oil in a pan and fry asafoetida, thyme and ginger for 1-2 minutes. Add beans, cover and cook on low heat for 15 minutes or till tender. Remove from heat, stir in salt, dried mango and red chilli.

KARELA AUR ALU
Bitter Gourd with Potatoes

Serves: 4

250 gm bitter gourd (karela)
1 tsp salt + ½ tsp turmeric
2 medium potatoes
100 gm (½ cup) ghee
Pinch asafoetida
½ tsp cumin seeds
1 tsp salt
½ tsp turmeric powder
2 tsp powdered aniseed (saunf)
2 tsp powdered coriander seeds
1½ tsp dried green mango powder (amchur)
1-2 green chillies, chopped

Scrape bitter gourds and rub with salt and turmeric mixture. Set aside for 2-3 hours.

Squeeze gourds to remove as much liquid as possible. Cook in plenty of boiling water for 10 minutes till tender-crisp. Drain and cut into pieces, discarding seeds.

Peel potatoes and cut into small pieces.

Heat ghee in a pan and fry asafoetida and cumin for 1-2 minutes. Add bitter gourds and potatoes and stir in remaining ingredients. Cover and cook on very low heat, stirring occasionally, for 30 minutes or till potatoes are tender.

BHARVA KARELA
Stuffed Bitter Gourd

Serves: 4

8 bitter gourds (karela)
1 tsp salt
2 tbsp ghee for cooking

Marinade:

200 gm (1½ cups) curd
1 tsp powdered red chilli
½ tsp turmeric powder
1 inch piece ginger, ground
6 cloves garlic, ground

Stuffing:

4 onions, grated
2 tbsp ghee
2 tbsp tamarind pulp
½ tsp salt

Bitter Gourd: Scrape bitter gourds, slit along one side and remove seeds. Put into a pan with one tsp salt, cover with cold water and bring to boil. Boil for 1-2 minutes, drain and squeeze out thoroughly to remove the bitter juice.

Marinade: Mix ingredients for marinade and set aside.

Stuffing: Heat 2 tbsp ghee in a pan and fry grated onions till pale gold. Remove from heat and add tamarind pulp and salt. Stuff bitter gourds with this mixture.

Rub prepared marinade over bitter gourds and leave for one hour.

Heat 2 tbsp ghee in a frying pan and place bitter gourds in a single layer.

Pour marinade on top, cover and cook on moderate heat turning once, till liquid dries and bitter gourds are golden.

BHARVA PARVAL
Stuffed Wax Gourd

Serves: 4-6

½ kg wax gourd (parval)
1 tsp salt
½ tsp turmeric powder
½ tsp powdered red chilli
1 tsp powdered aniseed (saunf)
1 tsp powdered coriander seeds
½ tsp powdered dried green mango (amchur)
2 tbsp grated fresh coconut
1 tbsp curd
100 gm (½ cup) ghee
Pinch asafoetida
½ tsp cumin seeds

Scrape parval and make a slit along the length of each.

Mix next eight ingredients together and stuff parval with this mixture.

Heat ghee in a pan and fry asafoetida and cumin for 1-2 minutes. Remove from heat, add parval and 50 ml water. Cover and cook on low heat for 20-30 minutes till parval is tender. Shake the pan occasionally during the cooking process.

BHARVA TINDA
Stuffed Round Squash

Serves: 4-5

½ kg tinda
1 tsp salt
½ tsp turmeric powder
½ tsp powdered red chilli
1 tsp powdered aniseed (saunf)
1 tsp powdered coriander seeds
½ tsp powdered dried green mango (amchur)
10-15 sultana (kishmish)
100 gm ghee
Pinch asafoetida
½ tsp cumin seeds

Peel tindas and cut a slice off the stalk end. Carefully scoop out pulp, keeping tindas whole. Chop pulp and mix in next seven ingredients. Stuff tindas with this mixture.

Heat ghee in a pan and fry asafoetida and cumin for 1-2 minutes.

Remove from heat and place tindas in pan in a single layer. Pour in 50 ml water, cover and cook on low heat for 20-30 minutes till tindas are tender. Shake the pan occasionally during cooking process.

BHARVA GHIA
Stuffed Marrow

Serves: 6-8

1 medium sized marrow, approx. 750 gm (ghia)

Stuffing:

2 tbsp ghee
200 gm (3 medium) onions, chopped
250 gm (2 medium) potatoes, boiled and roughly mashed
2 inch piece ginger, finely chopped
2-3 green chillies, finely chopped
2 tbsp chopped fresh coriander
1 tsp salt

Masala:

4 tbsp ghee
250 gm (4 medium) onions, grated
10 cloves garlic, ground
1 inch piece ginger, ground
1 tsp cumin seeds, roasted and ground
3 tsp powdered coriander seeds
½ tsp turmeric powder
1 tsp salt
500 gm (10 medium) tomatoes, skinned and chopped
Chopped fresh coriander to garnish

Cut off a thin slice along length of marrow. Carefully scoop out pulp, leaving a half inch rim all around. Chop pulp and reserve.

Stuffing: Heat 2 tbsp ghee in a pan and fry chopped onions till lightly coloured. Add chopped marrow pulp and cook for 3-5 minutes. Remove from heat and mix in mashed potatoes, ginger, green chillies, fresh coriander and salt.

Stuff marrow with mixture and keep aside.

Masala: Heat 4 tbsp ghee in a large pan and fry grated onions till golden. Stir in garlic, ginger, cumin, coriander powder, turmeric and salt. Cook and stir for 5 minutes, adding 1-2 tsp water from time to time. Add tomatoes and cook for 5-7 minutes till mixture is paste-like. Pour in 100 ml water and cook for a further 5-7 minutes.

Put stuffed marrow in masala, cover and cook on moderate heat for 20-30 minutes.

You can also put marrow into a greased baking dish, pour masala around it and bake in a moderate oven, 180 °C (350°F) for 30 minutes.

Sprinkle with chopped fresh coriander and serve.

GHIA KE KOFTE
Marrow Kofta

Serves: 6-8

Kofta:

1 kg marrow
2 tbsp gram flour (besan)
1 inch piece ginger, finely chopped
2-3 green chillies, finely chopped
2 tbsp chopped fresh coriander
250 gm (1¼ cups) ghee for frying

Gravy:

1 inch piece ginger
10 cloves garlic
1 tbsp coriander seeds
½ tsp cumin seeds
4 tbsp ghee
3 medium onions, grated
4 medium tomatoes, skinned and chopped
1½ tsp salt
100 gm (scant 1 cup) curd, whipped

Garnish:

2 tbsp chopped fresh coriander

Kofta: Peel marrow and grate. Mix in gram flour, ginger, coriander and chillies. Form into walnut sized balls.

Heat 250 gms ghee in a kadhai or deep frying pan and fry koftas till golden. Keep aside.

Gravy: Grind together ginger, garlic, coriander and cumin. Keep aside.

Heat 4 tbsp ghee in a pan and fry grated onions till golden. Stir in ground masala paste. Cook and stir 5 minutes, adding 1-2 tsp water from time to time. Add tomatoes and cook for a further 5-7 minutes till mixture is paste-like and ghee separates. Add salt and curd. Pour in 300 ml water. Simmer for 15 minutes.

Just before serving add koftas to gravy and simmer on low heat for 5-10 minutes. Sprinkle with fresh coriander and serve.

ZIMIKAND AUR MATAR
Elephant Foot Yam with Green Peas

Serves: 6-8

½ kg yam (zimikand)
1 kg green peas, shelled
200 gm (1 cup) ghee
Pinch asafoetida
½ tsp cumin seeds
½ tsp turmeric powder
½ tsp powdered red chilli
1 tsp powdered coriander seeds
2 tomatoes, chopped
1 tsp salt
100 gm (scant 1 cup) curd, whipped
1 tsp garam masala powder
½ tsp powdered dried green mango (amchur)

Peel yam and cut into largish pieces. Cook in plenty of boiling water till tender. Drain and cut into 1-1½ inch cubes.

Heat ghee in a pan and fry yam golden. Drain and keep aside.

Fry asafoetida and cumin in same ghee for 1-2 minutes. Stir in turmeric, chilli, coriander, salt and tomatoes and cook for a further 2-3 minutes. Add fried yam and peas. Pour in 250 ml water, cover and cook on low heat, stirring occasionally, for 15-20 minutes till vegetables are tender.

Add curd, garam masala and powdered green mango and cook for a further 10 minutes.

KATHAL
Jackfruit Curry

Serves: 4-5

½ kg jackfruit (kathal)
200 gm (1 cup) ghee
Pinch asafoetida
½ tsp cumin seeds
½ tsp turmeric powder
½ tsp powdered red chilli
1 tsp salt
1 tsp powdered coriander seeds
2 medium tomatoes, chopped
150 gm (⅔ cup) curd
1 tsp garam masala powder
½ tsp powdered dried green mango (amchur)

Using greased hands and a greased knife, peel jackfruit and cut into 1½ inch cubes. (You could get the greengrocer to do this for you.)

Peel seeds, being careful to remove every bit of peel as it can make the dish bitter.

Heat ghee in a pan and fry jackfruit (not seeds) till golden. Drain and keep aside.

In same ghee fry asafoetida and cumin for 1-2 minutes. Stir in turmeric, chilli, coriander, salt and tomatoes and cook for 2-3 minutes. Add fried jackfruit, seeds and 250 ml water. Cover and cook on low heat for 30 minutes till jackfruit is tender. Add whipped curd, garam masala and dried mango. Cook for 10-15 minutes more.

This can be served with either rice or chapati.

KADDU KI SABZI
Masala Pumpkin

Serves: 6

Try and get green pumpkin for this dish.

½ kg pumpkin
2 tbsp mustard oil
2 tsp chopped ginger
1-2 green chillies, chopped
Pinch asafoetida
½ tsp fenugreek seeds
Pinch powdered red chilli
1½ tsp salt
1 tsp sugar
1½ tsp powdered dried green mango (amchur)

Cut pumpkin into small pieces. (There is no need to peel green pumpkin. If using yellow pumpkin, peel it first.)

Heat oil in a kadhai or deep frying pan and fry ginger for 1-2 minutes. Stir in green chillies, asafoetida, fenugreek and red chilli. Fry for one minute. Add pumpkin, salt and sugar, cover and cook on low heat for 25-30 minutes till pumpkin is tender. Mash lightly, remove from heat and add dried green mango.

Rice

Rice is auspicious in all cultures. It is a symbol of fertility, prosperity and good fortune. Rice is offered to the gods, showered on newly married couples to wish them well and is the first cereal fed to an infant.

At Hindu weddings the brother of the bride gives her puffed rice to put into the sacred fire.

At Mathur weddings there is a ceremony called dhan bona (sowing of rice). After the wedding ceremony the newly wed couple sit together and all the bride's married relations go around them and shower them with rice. This is to wish them good fortune and prosperity and also presumably many children!

Sweet rice is particularly auspicious. Among the Bania community a new bride is welcomed with a dish of sweet rice. She shares this with seven suhagans (married women) before she enters her new home.

Muslims cook sweet rice at Id and other joyous occasions. Pulao and biryani is also made at Id and weddings. This combination of meat and rice is a particularly happy one—there are few things that match a good pulao.

In the old days anyone who was anyone lived in Chandni Chowk and many families had orchards in the outlying villages of Delhi. Often on a Sunday the whole family would set off for the orchard or bageechi, or sometimes to the Kutub Minar or Humayun's Tomb for the day. My father remembered the elders travelling by horse drawn carriages and the servants and children by bullock cart. Later of course, we all went by car.

On these occasions the food was carried from home except for the pulao, which was always cooked at the picnic site. I remember some of these picnics. My father's uncle would preside over the portable angeethi (coal brazier) and the huge pot of pulao—delicious and very rich. He used to say that unless there was an inch of ghee left in the pot after serving, the pulao was no pulao at all!

Men, incidentally, only ever cooked meat, leaving the vegetables to the women.

Pulao and Biryani are terms for a dish of rice cooked with meat. Rice and meat cooked together go back a long time and even find a mention in the Mahabharat. According to K.T. Achaya, 'Both Persian and Arabic are credited with the term pilav, pulao or pallao for the well known dish of rice cooked with spiced meat. Yet both Sanskrit and Tamil called the product pallao or pulao long before the Muslim advent.'

Biryani comes from the Persian word for rice, birinj.

To make pulao rice is cooked in mutton stock along with the cooked meat, whereas for biryani the rice is partly cooked in water and then combined with either cooked or raw, marinated meat and cooked together.

In Delhi pulao is considered the superior of the two and is by definition mutton pulao—there being no such thing as 'pea pulao.' Rice cooked with peas or any other vegetable is called *tahiri.*

Rice is very easy to cook if a few points are kept in mind.

Always use the best quality rice for pulao and wash in several changes of water.

Quantities of liquid needed for cooking rice can vary depending upon the quality of the rice, and on whether the rice has been pre-soaked or not. As a general rule the volume of water or stock should be double that of the rice. Another way is to measure the level of liquid above the surface of the rice—one inch if it has been soaked, and one and a half inches if it has not. I use the tried and tested method used by countless Indian cooks—dip your index finger into the pot so that the tip just touches the surface of the rice. The liquid should reach the level of the first joint for pre-soaked rice and one and a half joints for unsoaked rice. It never fails.

Cooked rice should be fluffy and the grains should be separate and should not have split.

When making mutton stock for pulao, cook the meat and bones over low heat for about two hours—the stock is ready when it is tacky to the touch.

SUNDAY PULAO
Rice Cooked with Mutton

Serves: 8-10

Stock:

1½ kg mutton pieces cut from shoulder or leg
2 tsp cumin seeds
1 tsp black peppercorn
10 cloves
2 pieces cinnamon, one inch each
6 black cardamoms
Pinch mace flakes
4 bay leaves
1 onion, quartered
1½ tsp salt

Rice:

1 kg (5 cups) basmati rice
400 gm (2 cups) ghee
2 medium onions, sliced
2 bay leaves
6 cloves
6-8 green cardamoms
2 inch piece ginger, finely chopped
10-12 cloves garlic, ground

Wash mutton, put into a pan and pour over 2 litres water. Tie all spices for stock in a piece of muslin and put into pan with onion and salt. Bring to boil, reduce heat and simmer for 1-1½ hours till meat is tender. Strain and keep stock aside. Discard spices and onion.

Wash rice thoroughly and soak in water for 20 minutes. Drain and keep for 10 minutes.

Heat ghee in a pan and fry sliced onions golden. Drain onions and keep aside.

Add bay leaves, cloves, cardamoms, ginger and garlic to the pan and fry for 1-2 minutes. Add cooked mutton and stir till lightly browned. Stir in drained rice and cook for 1-2 minutes. Measure 8-10 cups stock and pour into pan. (The level of stock should be one inch above surface of rice—you may need less than the measured amount).

Reduce heat, cover and cook for 20 minutes or till rice is tender and all stock has been absorbed.

Garnish with fried onions.

Sunday pulao is ideally served with kofta, bhunva kaleji, raita, and sweet mango chutney.

KORMA PULAO
Curried Mutton Pu

Serves: 10-12

1 kg (5 cups) basmati rice
1½ kg mutton pieces
250 gm (1¼ cup) ghee
250 gm (4 medium) onions, slice half and grind half
½ tsp ground nutmeg
2-3 blades mace
10-12 cloves
Seeds of 10 green cardamoms
1½ tsp salt
2 inch piece ginger, ground
10 cloves garlic, ground
½ tsp garam masala powder
Pinch powdered red chilli
200 ml milk

Wash and dry mutton.

Heat ghee in a pan and fry sliced onions till beginning to colour. Stir in nutmeg, mace, cloves and cardamom and fry till onions are golden.

Add mutton and salt and cook, adding a cupful of water a little at a time till mutton is half done (about 20-30 minutes).

Stir in ground onions, ginger, garlic, garam masala and red chilli. Add 250 ml water and cook stirring from time to time till mutton is tender and a rich brown.

Wash rice and soak for 20 minutes. Drain and leave for 10 minutes. Stir into cooked mutton. Add water to come one inch above surface of rice.

Cover and cook on low heat for 20-25 minutes. Sprinkle milk on rice, cover and put in a moderate oven, 150°C (350°F) for 10-15 minutes.

Serve with raita and onion relish.

TEH-B-TEH YAKHNI PULAO
Layered Mutton Pulao

Serves: 12-14

For this delicious layered pulao, one kg mutton is made into a korma for one layer, two kg is boiled for the stock and the best pieces from this are used for the other layer.

A recipe from *Rezia ka Shahi Dastarkhwana*.

1 kg (5 cups) basmati rice
3 kg mutton pieces
500 gm (2½ cups) ghee
100 gm (1 large) onion, sliced
50 gm (2½ inches) ginger, ground
2 + 2 heaped tbsp powdered coriander seeds
2 tsp salt
250 gm (2 cups) curd
Seeds of 16 green cardamoms, powdered
25 cloves, powdered
3-4 bay leaves
2 inch piece cinnamon
10 + 5 cloves, whole
1 tsp cumin seeds
4-5 black cardamoms
Pinch mace flakes
2 tsp salt
½ tsp saffron dissolved in 4-5 tsp water
½ tsp kewra essence

Clean and wash mutton.

Heat 250 gms (1¼ cups) ghee in a large pan and fry onions golden. Drain onions, grind and keep aside.

Put one kg mutton in the same pan and cook stirring for 10 minutes. Stir in half the ginger, 2 tbsp powdered coriander and 2 tsp salt. Pour in 500 ml water, cover and cook on low heat for 30-40 minutes. Add a little more water if necessary, and stir to prevent meat from sticking to bottom of pan. Stir in curd, ground fried onions and half powdered cloves and cardamom. Add 250 ml water and cook for a further 30 minutes till mutton is tender and liquid has dried. Keep aside.

Put remaining 2 kg mutton in a large pan. Tie bay leaves, cinnamon, 10 whole cloves, cumin, black cardamom and mace in a piece of muslin and put into the pan with mutton. Add 4 litres water and 2 tsp salt. Bring to boil, reduce heat, simmer uncovered for one and a half hours or till meat is tender. Discard bag of spices, drain mutton and keep aside. Measure stock and put into a pan. (You should have about 2½ litres of stock). Heat 50 gm (¼ cup) ghee, in a frying pan fry 5 cloves till black and pour into stock.

Wash rice and soak in water for 20 minutes. Drain and leave for 10 minutes.

Remove cloves from stock, bring to boil and add drained rice. Reduce heat, cover and cook for 12 minutes till rice is almost done. Keep aside.

From boiled mutton choose one kg of good pieces. Heat 150 gm (¾ cup) ghee in a large pan, put in mutton, remaining ginger, powdered cloves and cardamom and 2 tbsp coriander. Stir and cook for 1-2 minutes.

Put half the cooked rice on this mutton, sprinkle with a little saffron and kewra essence, and top with reserved mutton korma. Put remaining rice on korma, sprinkle saffron and kewra essence and pour 50 gm (¼ cup) melted ghee on top. Cover and seal lid with flour paste. Put on dum or in a very slow oven 150°C (300°F) for one hour.

Serve with raita.

MOTI PULAO
Pearl Pulao

Serves: 8-10

Tiny balls of mince covered with silver leaf (varak) make the moti
or pearls for this pulao.

Get the butcher to make very fine mince from a leg of mutton.
Keep the bones separate.

Stock:

Bones from the mutton
2 bay leaves
1 inch piece cinnamon
10 cloves
5 black cardamoms
½ tsp cumin seeds
½ tsp black peppercorn
Pinch mace flakes
1 tsp salt

Moti:

½ kg very fine mince
2 green chillies, finely chopped
1 tbsp chopped fresh coriander
½ tsp salt
1 egg, beaten
100 gm (½ cup) ghee for frying
Silver leaf (optional)

Rice:

½ kg (2½ cups) basmati rice
2 inch piece ginger, finely chopped
6-8 cloves garlic, ground
Pinch saffron, dissolved in 3-4 tsp water
Few drops kewra essence

Stock: Put mutton bones, bay leaves, whole spices and salt in a large pan. Cover with 1¾ litres water, bring to boil, reduce heat and simmer for 1-1½ hours. Strain and discard bones and spices. You should have about one litre of stock. Keep aside.

Moti: Mix mince with chillies, coriander, salt and egg and form into small balls the size of a pea. Heat 100 gm (½ cup) ghee in a frying pan and fry meatballs golden. Carefully open out a sheet of silver leaf, if using and roll balls of mince on it till covered. Keep aside.

Rice: Wash rice and soak for 20 minutes. Drain and leave for 10 minutes.

Heat remaining ghee in a pan and fry ginger and garlic for 1-2 minutes. Stir in rice and cook for 1-2 minutes. Pour in stock to come one inch above surface of rice, reduce heat, cover and cook for 15 minutes till rice is almost done.

Layer rice and meatballs in a greased pan, sprinkling a little saffron and kewra essence on each layer. (Begin and end with rice). Cover, seal lid with flour paste and put on dum or in a slow oven, 150°C (300°F) for 20-30 minutes.

MUTHANJAN PULAO
Sweet Mutton Pulao

Serves: 8-10

A recipe from the *Pukht-o-Paaz.*

This sweet pulao may not be to everybody's taste. You can leave out the sugar to get a pulao enriched with sultanas, almonds and milk.

1 kg mutton pieces
1 kg (5 cups) basmati rice
10 cloves
10 green cardamoms
1 inch piece cinnamon
1 tsp cumin seeds
½ tsp black peppercorn
1½ tsp salt
250 gm (1¼ cup) ghee
250 gm (4 medium) onions, sliced
4 inch piece ginger, finely sliced
3 tsp powdered coriander seeds
2 litres milk
250 gm (1¼ cups) almonds, blanched
250 gm (1¼ cups) sultanas (kishmish)
½ kg (2¼ cups) sugar
½ tsp saffron, dissolved in hot water

Wash mutton. Put into a large pan with 5 cloves, 5 cardamoms, cumin, peppercorns, cinnamon and salt. Pour in 3½ litres water, bring to boil, reduce heat and simmer for one and a half hours or till meat is tender. Drain meat and discard spices. Measure stock, which should be about 2-2½ litres. Heat 2 tbsp ghee, fry 5 cloves till black and pour into stock. Keep aside.

Heat remaining ghee and fry onions golden. Stir in ginger, coriander and 5 cardamoms and cook for 1-2 minutes. Add mutton, stir and cook till brown. Keep aside.

Meanwhile bring milk to boil, reduce heat and simmer till reduced to a quarter of its original volume. This will take about an hour. The milk will be very thick having a consistency of porridge.

Grind almonds with 100 ml stock and mix into thickened milk.

Wash rice and soak for 15 minutes. Drain. Leave for 10 minutes.

Remove cloves from stock, bring to boil and put in drained rice. Reduce heat, cover and cook for 12-15 minutes till rice is almost done and liquid is absorbed.

Put one third rice on top of cooked meat, spread with half milk mixture and scatter over half sultanas and sugar. Sprinkle with saffron. Add another third rice, remaining milk, sultanas and sugar and a little more saffron. Finally top with remaining rice and saffron. Cover and seal lid with flour paste and put on dum or in a slow oven, 150°C (300°F) for 20-30 minutes.

Stir gently to mix before serving.

Variation: Omit sugar and sprinkle ½ cup orange juice on each layer of rice along with milk and sultanas.

BABU SHAHI'S BIRYANI

Serves: 8-10

1 kg mutton pieces
1 kg (5 cups) basmati rice
250 gm (1¼ cup) ghee
50 gm (2 pods) garlic, ground
50 gm (2½ inches) ginger, finely sliced
½ tsp each cloves and black peppercorn
Seeds of 6 black cardamoms, crushed
2 pieces cinnamon, one inch each
4 bay leaves
1½ tsp salt
100 gm (scant 1 cup) curd
Pinch saffron, dissolved in 3-4 tsp hot water
Orange food colour (optional)

Heat ghee and fry garlic golden. Stir in ginger and spices and cook for 1-2 minutes. Add mutton and cook for 10-15 minutes till lightly browned.

Add curd, salt and 1½ litres water. Cook on medium heat for one hour or till meat is tender, adding more water if necessary. When meat is done there should be approximately 250 ml of liquid in the pan.

Wash rice and cook in plenty of water for 5-7 minutes till half done. Drain.

Put rice on top of cooked mutton and sprinkle with saffron. Sprinkle a few drops of food colour randomly over rice. Cover and seal lid with flour paste.

Put on very low heat or in a slow oven, 150°C (300°F) for 45 minutes.

Before serving stir biryani to mix rice and meat.
Serve with raita and onion relish.

Chicken Biryani can be made in a similar way. Use 1-2 chicken cut into 10 pieces each. Cook chicken for 20 minutes and use only one litre water.

BARE MIYA'S BIRYANI

Serves: 6-8

Bare Mia was a cook who came to our family from a princely household where he was exclusively in charge of making the kababs! However he was a very good cook and was soon making all the family recipes, and also parted with some of his own.

I kg mutton pieces
750 gm (3¾ cups) rice
2 keenus or oranges
250 gm (1¼ cups) ghee
8 green cardamoms
10 + 6 cloves
3 pieces cinnamon, 1 inch each
2-3 bay leaves
Pinch mace flakes
2 inch piece ginger, cut into fine shreds
200 gm (¾ cup) curd
3 tsp salt
Pinch saffron

Cut the peel of keenus or oranges in four sections. (Eat the fruit or keep for another use). Scrape away bitter white part with a knife and cut peel into fine long shreds. Keep aside.

In a large pan heat ghee and fry cardamoms, 10 cloves, cinnamon, bay leaves and mace for 1-2 minutes. Add ginger and fry for one minute. Add mutton and cook for 15 minutes, stirring occasionally till lightly coloured. Add curd, orange peel, salt and 1½ litres water. Cook, uncovered on moderate heat for 1-1½ hours or till meat is tender. There should be approximately 750 ml of liquid in the pan.

Wash rice. Put into a large pan of cold water with 6 cloves. Bring to boil and cook for 3-5 minutes. Drain and discard water.

Put rice over cooked meat and mix gently. Dissolve saffron in 2-3 tsp hot water and sprinkle on top. Cover pan and seal with flour paste. Put on dum or very slow oven, 150°C (300°F) for 45 minutes.

Stir biryani gently before serving to mix meat and rice.

Serve with raita and onion relish.

MURGH PULAO
Chicken Pulao

Serves: 6-8

2 chicken, (1 kg each) cut into 10 pieces each
¾ kg (3¾ cups) basmati rice
2-3 bay leaves
2 inch piece cinnamon
6 black cardamoms
6 cloves
½ tsp black peppercorn
½ tsp cumin seeds
250 gm (1¼ cups) ghee
2 medium onions, sliced
10 cloves garlic, ground
1 inch piece ginger, finely chopped
2 tsp powdered coriander seeds
6 cloves, powdered
6 green cardamoms
100 gm (scant ½ cup) curd
1½ tsp salt

Wash chicken. Put neck, back and giblets in a pan with bay leaves,
cinnamon, black cardamoms, cloves, peppercorns and cumin.
Pour in 2 litres water, bring to boil, reduce heat and simmer for
one hour. Strain and discard bones and spices. Measure stock and
keep aside.

Wash rice and soak for 20 minutes. Drain and keep aside
while you cook chicken.

Heat ghee and fry onions golden. Stir in garlic, ginger,
powdered coriander and cloves and cook for 1-2 minutes. Add
green cardamoms, curd and salt and cook for 5-7 minutes. Add

chicken pieces and cook for 10 minutes till chicken is brown and liquid is dry.

Stir in rice, cook for 1-2 minutes. Pour in enough chicken stock to come one inch above surface of rice. Cover and cook on low heat for 20 minutes till rice and chicken are tender.

Serve with raita and sweet mango chutney.

MAHI PULAO
Fish Pulao

Serves: 6-8

A recipe from the *Pukht-o-Paaz.*

To remove the fishy smell, 'wash' the fish first with ground black cumin seeds, then ground aniseed, then mustard oil and finally with gram flour.

This process was relevant in the days before refrigeration. Now that very fresh fish is available it can be omitted.

1 kg fish pieces, prepared as above
½ kg (2½ cups) basmati rice
250 gm (1 cup) ghee
250 gm (4 medium) onions, sliced
10-12 cloves garlic, ground
2 inch piece ginger, ground
2 tbsp powdered coriander seeds
1 tsp salt
200 gm (1¾ cups) curd, whipped
6 cloves, powdered
Seeds of 6 green cardamoms, powdered
6 each whole cloves and green cardamoms

In a large pan, heat 200 gm (1 cup) ghee and fry sliced onions golden. Drain and keep aside. Stir garlic, ginger and coriander into same ghee and cook for 1-2 minutes. Remove from heat. Add salt, curd and powdered cloves and cardamoms. Crumble in fried onions, return to heat and cook for 5-7 minutes. Add fish, cover and cook for 5-7 minutes till fish is firm. Take pan off heat and keep aside.

165

Wash rice. Cook in plenty of water with whole cloves and cardamoms for 12-15 minutes till almost done. Drain rice and put on top of cooked fish. Melt remaining ghee and pour on top. Cover and seal lid with flour paste. Put on dum or in a slow oven, 150°C (300°F) for 30-40 minutes.

MATAR KI TAHIRI
Rice Cooked with Green Peas

Serves: 6-8

½ kg (2½ cups) basmati rice
300 gm shelled green peas
2 onions, quartered
1 tsp black peppercorn
½ tsp cloves
5 black cardamoms
2 inch piece cinnamon
2-3 bay leaves
2 tsp salt
200 gm (1 cup) ghee
1 tsp cumin seeds

Boil peas in plenty of water till tender. Drain peas and reserve water. To this water add onions, all the spices and salt. Simmer for 15-20 minutes. Strain, discard spices and keep water.

Wash rice and soak for 20 minutes. Drain. Leave for 10 minutes.

Heat ghee and fry cumin seeds for 1-2 minutes. Stir in peas and rice and cook for 1-2 minutes.

Pour in reserved spice stock to come one inch above surface of rice. (Add more water if necessary). Cover and cook on low heat for 15-20 minutes till rice is done.

Serve with raita and green chutney.

Variation:
Boot ki Tahiri: This can be made in the same way, substituting 250 gm fresh green gram for the peas.

CHANE KI DAL KI TAHIRI
Rice Cooked with Bengal Gram

Serves: 6-8

200 gm (1 cup) Bengal gram (chana dal)
½ kg (2½ cups) rice
200 gm (1 cup) ghee
2 bay leaves
10 cloves
6-8 green cardamoms
2 one inch pieces cinnamon
½ tsp black peppercorn
1½ tsp salt

Wash and soak dal for 8-10 hours. Drain and leave for 10 minutes.

Wash and soak rice for 15-20 minutes. Drain. Leave for 10 minutes.

Heat ghee in a pan and fry bay leaves and spices for 1-2 minutes. Stir in dal, reduce heat, cover and cook for 5 minutes.

Add rice and salt, stir one minute then pour in enough water to come one inch above surface of rice.

Cover and cook on low heat for 20 minutes till rice and dal are tender.

Discard bay leaves and cinnamon before serving.

KHILVA KHICHRI
Dry Khichri

Serves: 6-8

250 gm (1¼ cups) rice
200 gm (2 cups) split green beans (chhilke ki mung ki dal)
100 gm (½ cup) ghee
1 tsp cumin seeds
2 bay leaves
10 cloves
½ tsp black peppercorn
250 gm button onions
2 tsp salt

Wash rice and dal, combine and soak in cold water for 20 minutes. Drain and keep for 10 minutes.

Heat ghee in a pan and fry cumin seeds, bay leaves, cloves and peppercorn for 1-2 minutes. Add button onions and fry one minute. Stir in rice and dal, cook for 1-2 minutes, add salt and pour in enough water to come 1½ inches above surface of khichri. Cover and cook on low heat for 20 minutes till rice and dal are tender. Discard bay leaves before serving.

Serve with raita and sweet mango chutney.

ZARDA PULAO
Sweet Rice

Serves: 6-8

The Zard Birinj mentioned in the *Ain-I-Akbari* is made of:

10 s. rice, 5 s. sugar candy, 3½ s. ghi, ½ s. each of sultanas, almonds and pistachios, ¼ s. of salt, ⅛ s. of fresh ginger, 1½ d. saffron, 2½ m. of cinnamon—where s is seer or approximately 1 kg, d is dam or 20 gm and m is mishqual or 96 barley grains.

The following recipe is a slight modification of the above, reducing proportions to one tenth.

250 gm (1¼ cups) rice
100 gm (½ cup) ghee
2 inch piece cinnamon
½ tsp finely chopped ginger
8 green cardamoms, roughly pounded
25 gm (2 tbsp) each sultana (kishmish), almonds and pistachio nuts
200 gm (1 cup) sugar
Good pinch saffron, dissolved in 4 –5 tsp hot water
Few drops yellow food colour
2-3 drops kewra essence

Wash rice thoroughly and soak for 20 minutes in double its volume of water. Drain and reserve water.

Heat ghee in a pan and fry cinnamon, ginger and cardamoms for 2-3 minutes. Add raisins, sliced almonds and pistachio nuts and fry further for 1-2 minutes. Stir in drained rice and cook for 1-2 minutes, pour in reserved water, cover and cook on low heat for 15 minutes.

Remove from heat, add sugar, saffron and food colour if using. Stir gently to distribute sugar.

Return to low heat and cook for 5-10 minutes till rice is tender. Sprinkle with kewra essence mixed with a little water.

Roti

For want of another word roti, parantha, naan etc. are referred to as 'Indian Bread'. Most 'breads' in India are flat and non-leavened, and are cooked on a griddle or deep-fried. Although some are leavened and even cooked in a traditional Indian oven (tandoor), they are still flat and very different from the European bread, which is allowed to double in bulk before baking. (Hence the name, 'Double Roti').

PHULKA

Makes: 20-25

The simplest of breads is the phulka, so called because it puffs up when cooked.

3 cups wholewheat flour (atta)
approx. 1½ cups water
Extra wholewheat flour for rolling

Sieve flour into a flat pan or thali. Gradually add most of the water and mix to a soft dough. Knead and fold dough for 7-10 munutes, sprinkling remaining water during the process. Cover with a damp cloth and leave for 30 minutes.

Knead again thoroughly. Pinch off small pieces of dough, make into balls and flatten on your palms using a little dry flour. Roll out thinly into 5 inch circles, using more dry flour to prevent sticking.

Heat griddle and cook phulka on medium heat for one minute

on each side, till dry and beginning to brown. Remove griddle from fire. Using tongs, place phulka on direct flame for a few seconds till it puffs up. Turn and cook other side. Serve immediately.

To make a karara (crisp) phulka keep on direct flame a little longer, till burnt patches appear. These semi-burnt phulkas are delicious with dal or with a little butter.

KHAMEERI ROTI STARTER
Leavened Bread Starter

There are several ways of making the khameer or starter, of which two are given below.

Method 1:

100 gm (scant 1 cup) flour (maida)
60 gm (8 tbsp) curd
Seeds of 4 green cardamoms, powdered
½ tsp grated nutmeg
2 tsp baking soda
2 tbsp sugar

Mix all ingredients together, add enough water to make a thick batter and beat till frothy.

Cover and leave for one day before using.

Method 2:

100 gm (scant 1 cup) flour (maida)
30 gm (2 tbsp) sour curd
½ tsp powdered aniseed (saunf)
2 tbsp sugar

Mix all ingredients together, add enough water to make a thick batter and beat well.

Cover and leave for one day before using.
The starter can be refrigerated for a day or two and used as required.

KHAMEERI ROTI
Leavened Bread

Makes: 40-50

1 kg wholewheat flour (atta)
60 gm (one third of above portion) starter
1 tsp salt
1¼ litres warm milk

Mix starter and salt into flour. Add milk and knead thoroughly.
Cover and keep aside for 1-2 hours.

Knead again with greased hands. Pinch off small pieces of
dough, roll in a little dry flour and form into chapatis with hands,
or roll out slightly thicker than for phulka.

Cook each side for a few minutes on a griddle on low heat then
put on direct flame till puffed.

POORI
Deep-fried Bread

Makes: 10-12

250 gm (2 cups) wholewheat flour (atta)
Pinch salt
Approx. 150 ml water
500 gm (2½ cups) ghee for frying

Sift flour and salt. Add water a little at a time to make a soft dough. Knead thoroughly for 10-15 minutes. Cover with damp cloth and leave for half an hour.

Using greased hands make walnut sized rounds of dough and roll out thinly.

Heat ghee in a kadhai or wok till smoking, reduce heat and gently lower 2-3 pooris at a time into ghee. Fry till golden and puffed.

Variations:

Mix 250 gm cooked and pureed spinach, or 250 gm cooked and pureed beetroot with flour, and make dough using water as required. Knead and proceed as for plain pooris.

BERVIN POORI
Poori Stuffed with Black Gram

Makes: 10-12

Bervin poori, potatoes and halva is a favourite holiday breakfast.

Dough as for plain poori made of 250 gm wholewheat flour (see previous recipe)

Filling:
125 gm (⅔ cup) husked black beans (dhuli urad ki dal)
2 tsp finely chopped ginger
3 tsp coriander seeds, crushed
1 tsp aniseed (saunf)
½ tsp powdered red chilli
2 tsp chopped fresh coriander
500 gm (2½ cups) ghee for frying

Soak dal in water for 8-10 hours. Drain and grind to a fine, fairly stiff paste. Mix in remaining ingredients.

Take some dough and shape into a small circle with your hands. Put one level tsp dal mixture in the centre and fold over dough to enclose filling completely.

Roll out carefully and fry in hot ghee as for pooris.

BESANI POORI
Deep-Fried Gram Flour Bread

Makes: 10-12

200 gm (2 cups) gram flour (besan)
125 gm (1 cup) wholewheat flour (atta)
½ tsp salt
¼ tsp powdered red chilli
2 tsp chopped fresh fenugreek leaves
Pinch asafoetida
500 gm (2½ cups) ghee for frying

Sieve together all dry ingredients. Add cold water a little at a time and mix to a fairly stiff dough. Cover and leave for 30 minutes.

Pinch off walnut sized pieces of dough and roll out thinly. Fry in hot ghee till puffed up and golden.

Besani Roti

Add 2 tbsp chopped onions to dough. Roll out and put roti on a hot griddle. With the point of a sharp knife prick roti all over to prevent it from rising. Cook for one minute then turn on the other side till cooked through.

MAMOOLI BIRAI ROTI
Ordinary Stuffed Bread

Makes: 16

A recipe from the *Pukht-o-Paaz.*

1 kg flour or wholewheat flour
1 tsp salt
125 gm (⅔ cup) ghee

Filling:

375 gm Bengal gram (chana dal)
½ tsp salt
Pinch pepper

Sieve flour and salt. Rub in ghee and add enough water to make a soft, not sticky dough. Knead thoroughly, cover with damp cloth and keep aside for one hour.

Cook dal till tender and dry. Mash thoroughly. Add salt and pepper.

Divide dough into 16 equal parts. Roll into balls and flatten to make small circles. Put a little dal into the centre, fold over to enclose filling, then shape into a chapati with hands.

Cook on a medium hot griddle, turning twice till cooked through.

KHAS BIRAI ROTI
Special Stuffed Bread

Makes: 16

A recipe from the *Pukht-o-Paaz*.

>1 kg flour (maida)
>1 tsp salt
>500 gm (2½ cups) ghee

Filling one:

>375 gm (1¾ cups) Bengal gram (chana dal)
>4 tbsp ghee
>½ tsp salt
>Pinch pepper

Sieve flour and salt. Rub in ghee. Use enough water to make a soft dough and leave aside for one hour.

Fry dal in 4 tbsp ghee. Add water and cook till tender and dry. Grind and add salt and pepper. Use to stuff rotis.

Make rotis as in previous recipe.

Filling two:

>375 gm shelled pistachio nuts
>Salt and pepper

Boil the pistachio nuts, peel and grind finely. Season and use to stuff rotis.

Make rotis as in previous recipe.

Filling three:

>1½ kg (12 cups) curd
>4 cloves

Seeds of 4 green cardamoms
Pinch mace flakes
Salt and pepper

Tie curd in muslin and hang for 2–2½ hours till it is the consistency of cream cheese. Grind cloves, cardamoms and mace and mix into curd with salt and pepper. Use to stuff rotis.

Make rotis as in previous recipe.

BAKARKHANI
Bakarkhan's Bread

Makes: 12-14

Bakarkhani, also called sheermal is reportedly named after Bakarkhan, one time governor of Bengal.
This rich and very special roti is served with korma and roghanjosh and is quite delicious even on its own.

It is made in a tandoor (a traditional Indian oven). Reasonable results can be obtained using a griddle, but a western style oven is not recommended.

From the *Pukht-oPaaz*

1 kg fine flour (maida)
750 ml milk
1 tsp salt
3 tbsp sugar
200 gm (1 cup) ghee
1 egg white
2 tbsp milk
Extra melted ghee

Sieve flour with salt and mix in sugar.

Heat milk till tepid and mix into flour. Leave for 3 hours in a warm place.

Melt ghee and mix into flour mixture. (At this stage the dough is very sticky.) Turn out dough onto a floured surface and knead thoroughly, lifting it and slapping it down till it becomes smooth and elastic. This will take 15-20 minutes and you may need to sprinkle a little extra flour during the process.

Form into ¼ inch thick rotis with hands and prick all over with fork.

Cook in a tandoor or on a moderately hot griddle till golden on both sides. Mix egg white with milk and brush on hot roti. Cook for a few minutes more.

Brush with melted ghee and serve.

PARANTHA

Makes: 6-8

2 cups wholewheat flour (atta) + extra for dusting
¾-1 cup water
8 tbsp ghee, melted

Sieve flour into a flat pan or thali. Gradually add enough water to
make a soft dough. Knead and fold dough sprinkling water during
the process. Knead thoroughly for 10-15 minutes, cover with a
damp cloth and leave for 30 minutes.

Pinch off a walnut sized piece of dough, form into a ball and
flatten on the palm of your hand. Using a little dry flour roll into a
5-6 inch circle. Brush with a little melted ghee. Fold into a
semi-circle, brush again with ghee and fold to make a triangle.
Press firmly and roll out into a large triangle.

Heat griddle on medium heat and place parantha on it. Using
the back of a spoon rub ghee on parantha and drizzle some all
around edges. Turn after one minute and rub ghee on other side.
Cook till parantha is crisp and golden on both sides. Make
remaining paranthas in the same way.

ALU KA PARANTHA
Potato Filled Parantha

Makes: 6

Dough as for plain paranthas (See previous recipe)
6 tbsp ghee, melted

Filling:

2 large potatoes, boiled and mashed
1 medium onion, finely chopped
1 tbsp chopped fesh coriander
1-2 green chillies, finely chopped
1 tsp dried green mango powder (amchur)
1 tsp salt

Mix together all ingredients for the filling.

Flatten a piece of dough on your palm, place a little filling in the centre and press dough around to enclose. Using a little dry flour roll out into a 5 inch circle. Cook as for plain parantha.

Variation:

Matar ka Parantha: Replace the potatoes with one cup boiled, mashed green peas.

Gobi ka Parantha: Use one small uncooked cauliflower, grated, instead of potatoes.

KATLUMA PARANTHA
Layered Parantha

Makes: 8-10

250 gm (2 cups) flour (maida)
¼ tsp salt
250-300 ml water
6 level tbsp ghee + 200 gm (1 cup) for frying
2 tbsp flour

Sieve 250 gms flour and salt. Gradually add enough water to make a soft dough. Cover with damp cloth and keep aside for half an hour.

Melt ghee and knead 2 tbsp into dough, till soft and elastic. To the remaining ghee add 2 tbsp flour and mix to a paste.

Divide dough into 8-10 equal parts. Flatten with hands to make a small circle then roll out thinly and fold in half. Spread with a little flour paste and fold lengthwise in half again. Roll this strip like a pinwheel, keeping the folded edges outward and forming a cone shape. Press with hands to flatten. Form into a chapati with hands.

Heat a little ghee on a griddle and fry parantha trickling ghee a little at a time down sides of griddle. Turn once and cook till golden on both sides.

Desserts and Sweets

Indians have a very sweet tooth and people from Delhi are no exception. There is a variety of mithais and sweets available at the many sweet shops and vendors all over the city. Till about thirty years ago a man used to come around in Old Delhi selling the most delicious malai ki baraf—a cross between icecream and kulfi. In winter an old woman came with a basket of daulat ki chaat—a heavenly confection of milk foam. Festivals meant baskets layered with different sweets and as children it was a joy to remove each layer and see which mithai was next. A cardboard box is not the same thing at all! At weddings the halwais came to the house and delighted us with freshly made barfis, laddoos and desserts like kheer and phirni.

In the following recipes the quantity of sugar can be adjusted to suit individual tastes.

KHEER
Rice Cooked in Milk

Serves: 6

Kheer is a sweet made of milk cooked with rice or some other ingredient such as vermicelli, carrots, pumpkin, bottle gourd, lotus seed and almost anything that takes your fancy. When these are cooked in milk and sweetened you get vermicelli kheer or carrot kheer etc. But when the word kheer is used on its own it generally refers to rice cooked in milk.

This sweet is particularly auspicious and associated with a number of ceremonies. It is also the first solid food given to a baby.

Among the Khatris the cooked kheer is stirred in the moonlight on Sharad Purnima, the full moon just before Diwali. The light of this particular moon is considered the most cooling and beneficial for the brain and the eyes. The kheer, when stirred supposedly absorbs these properties, and imparts them to the person who eats it.

Another custom associated with Sharad Purnima is that of threading a needle. All the ladies of the household gather together and each holds a needle against the full moon and threads it. This is supposed to improve the eyesight, though one needs fairly good eyes in the first place if one is to achieve the objective!

50 gm (3 heaped tbsp) rice
1 litre milk
100 gm (½ cup) sugar
25 gm (approx. 20) almonds, blanched and sliced

25 gm (2 tbsp) sultanas (kishmish)
Seeds of 4-5 green cardamoms, powdered

Wash rice and soak in cold water for one hour.

Heat milk in a pan add drained rice and cook on low heat, stirring frequently till thickened.

Remove from heat, add sugar and stir till dissolved. Stir in almonds, sultanas and powdered cardamom.

Serve hot or cold.

Note: Be very careful when re-heating kheer or any other milk based sweet as it burns very easily. Stir constantly to prevent it sticking to the pan and burning. Unattended kheer can burn in a second and acquire an unpleasant smoky flavour.

MAKHANE KI KHEER
Lotus Seed Kheer

Serves: 6

50 gm dried lotus seed (makha
1 litre milk
100 gm (½ cup) sugar
25 gm (approx. 20) almonds, blanched and sliced
25 gm (2 tbsp) sultanas (kishmish)
Seeds of 4-5 green cardamoms, powdered
Pinch saffron, dissolved in 3-4 tsp hot water
2 tsp rosewater

Remove any hard black bits from lotus seeds and cut each into four pieces. Toast lightly on a griddle for 1-2 minutes.

Heat milk in a pan add lotus seeds and cook on low heat, stirring from time to time till thickened.

Remove from heat, add sugar and stir till dissolved.

Stir in almonds, sultanas, cardamom, saffron and rosewater.

This kheer is best served chilled.

BAJRE KI KHEER
Pearl Millet Kheer

Serves: 6-8

50 gm (3 heaped tbsp) millet grains (bajra grains)
1 tbsp ghee
1 litre milk
100 gm (½ cup) sugar
Pinch saffron

Heat ghee in a pan and fry millet for 1-2 minutes.

Bring milk to boil, add millet and reduce heat. Cook on low heat, stirring occasionally, for 40-50 minutes till thickened. Remove from heat, add sugar and stir to dissolve. Dissolve saffron in 2-3 tsp water and stir into kheer.

This can be served either chilled or hot. Re-heat carefully.

BADAAM KI KHEER
Almond Kheer

Serves: 4-6

200 gm (1 cup) almonds, blanched and sliced
1 litre milk
100 gm (½ cup) sugar
Seeds of 4-5 green cardamoms, powdered

Put milk into a pan, bring to boil, reduce heat and simmer for 15-20 minutes till thickened.

Add sliced almonds and cook for a further 10 minutes. Remove from heat, add sugar and stir to dissolve. Stir in powdered cardamom.

This kheer is served warm to a nursing mother, but can also be chilled before serving.

GULATHI
Fried Kheer

Serves: 15-20

A recipe from *Pukht-o-Paaz*. This 'fried' kheer is served at Muslim weddings, and is more akin to a halva.

Although this recipe sounds extremely rich, the finished product does not feel heavy whilst eating.

250 gm (1¼ cups) basmati rice
5 green cardamoms
5 cloves
2 litres milk
375 gm (1¾ cups) top of milk (balai)
250 gm (1¼ cups) ghee
500 gm (2½ cups) sugar
125 gm (⅔ cup) almonds, blanched and sliced
½ tsp kewra essence
Silver leaf (varak) and sliced pistachio nuts to decorate

Wash rice and soak in cold water for one hour. Drain and boil in a pan in plenty of water with cardamoms and cloves for 10-12 minutes. Drain and discard spices.

Put semi-cooked rice into a large pan with milk, top of milk and ghee. Bring to boil, reduce heat and simmer till thick. This will take about 20 minutes.

Add sugar, stir and mash rice against sides of pan till sugar is dissolved and mixture is very thick. Stir in almonds and kewra essence. Turn out onto a plate to cool and set.

Decorate with silver leaf and pistachio nuts before serving.

PHIRNI
Ground Rice Sweet

Serves: 6-8

Phirni is the crème-de-la-crème of rice sweets. It has a creamy consistency and a delicate flavour which is enhanced by serving the phirni in individual shakoras—unglazed earthenware pots.

50 gm (3 heaped tbsp) rice
1 litre milk
175 gm (scant 1 cup) sugar
Seeds of 8 green cardamoms, powdered
2-3 drops kewra essence
25 gm (2 tbsp) pistachio nuts, sliced

Wash rice thoroughly and soak in cold water for 2-3 hours. Drain rice and keep water.

Grind rice to a very fine paste, using some reserved water.

Bring milk just to boiling. Remove from heat, stir in rice paste and mix thoroughly.

Return pan to very low heat and cook, stirring constantly. (It is important not to let your attention wander as the mixture may become lumpy or burn.)

Keep stirring and cooking for 15-20 minutes till mixture thickens and coats back of spoon. Cook for 2-3 minutes more. Remove from heat add sugar and stir to dissolve—mixture will get slightly thin but do not worry.

Stir in cardamom and kewra essence.

Pour into a dish, cool and sprinkle with pistachio nuts. Chill till ready to serve.

If using unglazed earthenware pots, soak these in cold water for 1-2 hours. Drain and allow water to drip away. Spoon some cooled phirni into each pot and sprinkle pistachio nuts on top. Chill and serve.

SHEER KHURMA-I
Vermicelli Cooked in Milk

Serves: 30

This milk and vermicelli kheer is made at Meethi Id after Ramzan. It can be as simple or as rich as you like. According to Babu Shahi, the wealthy people enrich the sheer khurma with khoya (dried unsweetened condensed milk), nuts and sultanas, whilst the not so well off make do with a simple vermicelli kheer.

Babu Shahi's version of Sheer Khurma

5 litres milk
100 gm (½ cup) ghee
100 gm vermicelli
250 gm khoya, (dried unsweetened condensed milk) crumbled
50 gm (5 tbsp) chironji
50 gm (4 tbsp) sultanas (kishmish)
50 gm almonds, (⅓ cup) peeled and sliced
1 kg sugar
Few drops kewra essence

In a large pan bring milk to boil, reduce heat and simmer for 15-20 minutes till slightly thickened.

Heat ghee in a kadhai or wok and fry vermicelli till golden.

Drain vermicelli and put into milk along with khoya, chironji, sultanas and almonds. Cook for 15-20 minutes more, stirring frequently till thick and creamy.

Remove from heat add sugar and stir till dissolved. Stir in kewra essence.

Chill and serve.

Note: Sheer Khurma can also be made using 100 gm (½ cup) rice instead of vermicelli.

SHEER KHURMA-2
Vermicelli Cooked in Milk

Serves: 12

A recipe from *Rezia ka Shahi Dastarkhwana*

250 gm fine vermicelli
2 litres milk
60 gm (4 tbsp) ghee
8 dried dates (chhurara), de-seeded and chopped
25 gm chironji
300 gm (1½ cups) sugar
25 gm (approx. 20) almonds, sliced
Seeds of 6 green cardamoms, powdered

Roast vermicelli on a griddle till light brown. (It is possible to buy pre-roasted vermicelli, in which case this step is not necessary). Keep aside.

Bring milk to boil in a large pan, reduce heat and simmer for 15-20 minutes till slightly thickened.

While milk is simmering, heat ghee in a frying pan and fry dates and chironji for 2-3 minutes. Drain and keep aside.

When milk is ready, gently stir in vermicelli along with fried dates and chironji. Cook for 10 minutes.

Remove from heat, add sugar and stir to dissolve. Stir in almonds and powdered cardamom.

The consistency of this sheer khurma is quite thin.

Chill and serve.

SHEERE KI SEVIAN
Vermicelli in Milk

Serves: 10-12

A recipe from the *Pukht-o-Paaz.*

250 gm fine vermicelli
150 gm (¾ cup) ghee
500 gm (2½ cups) sugar
Few drops yellow food colouring (optional)
5-6 cloves, ground
Seeds of 6 green cardamoms, ground
2-3 drops kewra essence
125 ml milk
20 pistachio nuts, sliced
Silver leaf (varak)

Roast vermicelli on a moderately hot griddle till pale gold. (Not necessary if you are using the pre-roasted variety.)

Tie vermicelli loosely in a piece of muslin.

Have ready a large pan of boiling water. Dip bundle of vermicelli quickly in this, holding it down with a spoon just for a few seconds. Take out and dip twice more.

Open bundle and put vermicelli into a large pan.

In a small pan, melt half the ghee and pour on top of vermicelli. Mix gently, cover and leave for 10 minutes.

Add sugar and put pan on a very gentle heat. Shake pan from time to time till sugar is dissolved. Remove from heat and leave for 10 minutes.

Add cloves, cardamoms, kewra essence and milk. If using

colour, add to milk. Pour in remaining ghee and return pan to gentle heat. Cover and cook for 10-15 minutes till milk is absorbed.

Turn out onto a plate and decorate with silver leaf and sliced pistachio nuts.

MUZAAFAR
Dry Vermicelli

Serves: 10-12

A recipe from *Rezia ka Shahi Dastarkhwana*

250 gm fine vermicelli
250 gm (1¼ cups) ghee
500 ml milk
500 gm (2½ cups) sugar
2-3 drops kewra essence
250 gm khoya, (dried unsweetened condensed milk) crumbled or grated
25 gm (approx. 20) almonds, sliced

Heat ghee in a kadhai or deep frying pan and fry vermicelli in 5-6 batches, till light brown. (If you are using pre-roasted vermicelli, fry each batch for 1-2 minutes.) Drain vermicelli on kitchen paper and put into a large pan.

Heat milk just to boiling and pour over fried vermicelli. Press gently with a spoon so that all the vermicelli is moistened. Cover and leave to soak for 10 minutes.

Put sugar into a separate pan with 100 ml water. Stir over gentle heat till sugar is dissolved, then boil rapidly for one minute. Pour sugar syrup over vermicelli and milk mixture and put pan on a very gentle heat. Cover and cook undisturbed for 15-20 minutes till liquid has been absorbed.

Each strand of vermicelli should be separate.

Add kewra essence and khoya and turn carefully with a fork to mix.

Turn out into a dish and sprinkle with almonds. Serve cold.

PAGGI SEVIAN
Sugared Vermicelli

Serves: 5-6

This crisp vermicelli is made at the festival of raksha bandhan, the festival for brothers and sisters.

200 gm white vermicelli
5 level tbsp ghee (no substitute)
200 gm (1 cup) caster sugar

Heat ghee in a kadhai or wok and fry vermicelli on moderate heat till golden. Add sugar, flick in a little water with your fingers and stir till vermicelli is coated with sugar. Work quickly as sugar should not caramelise. Turn out into a plate and cool. Break into pieces. Store in an airtight container.

SHAHI TUKRA
Bread Sweet

Serves: 6-8

6 slices white bread
200 gm (1 cup) ghee
2 litres milk
200 gm (1 cup) sugar
25 gm (2 tbsp) sultanas (kishmish)
2-3 drops kewra essence
Seeds of 5 green cardamoms, ground
25 gm (approx. 20) almonds, sliced

Remove crusts from bread and cut each slice in half.

Heat ghee and fry bread, turning once till golden on both sides. Keep aside.

In a large pan bring milk to boil, lower heat and cook till reduced by almost half. Remove from heat and stir in sugar. Put in fried bread and cook on gentle heat for 5-10 minutes. With a perforated spoon carefully transfer bread to a shallow dish and scatter with sultanas.

Stir kewra and cardamoms into milk and pour over bread. Sprinkle with sliced almonds.

Chill and serve.

RABRI
Thickened Milk Sweet

Serves: 6-8

2 litres full cream milk
150 gm (¾ cup) sugar
Seeds of 4-5 green cardamoms, powdered
1 tsp rosewater, or 2-3 drops kewra essence
15-20 almonds, blanched and sliced
15-20 pistachio nuts, blanched and sliced

Put milk in a kadhai or wok and bring to boil. Reduce heat and simmer, stirring from time to time till milk is very thick and reduced to a third or a quarter of original volume. (Keep scraping the skin, which sticks to the sides of the pan, and stir it in). This will take 1-1½ hours. Remove from heat, add sugar and stir to dissolve. Stir in powdered cardamom, essence, almonds and pistachio nuts. Chill before serving.

Desserts and Sweets

KHURCHAN
Layered Cream Sweet

Serves: 4-6

The word khurchan means 'scrapings'. It is made of layers of malai (top of milk), sweetened and flavoured and is best had when fresh, as it is very perishable.

There is a shop in Kinari Bazar where you get delicious khurchan if you are there at the right time—which varies from day to day! However, with a little practice and a great deal of patience you can make it at home.

A large shallow kadhai or wok (NOT nonstick as the skin from the milk has to stick to the sides) is essential for the success of this sweet.

2 litres full cream milk
100 gm (½ cup) castor sugar
2 tsp rosewater
25 gm (2 tbsp) pistachio nuts, blanched and sliced
Shallow dish, approx. 7 inches in diametre

Put milk into a large shallow kadhai or wok. Bring to boil, stir and allow to come to boil once more. Reduce heat slightly and continue to cook. When a layer of skin forms on top, gently push it to one side with a wooden spatula and stick it to side of kadhai. Continue sticking each layer of skin as it forms to sides of kadhai till all the milk is used up. The whole process will take 1-1½ hours.

(Do not let it get brown—khurchan is very pale cream in colour).

Remove kadhai from heat.

Put sugar into a small pan with 4 tbsp water and stir over gentle heat till dissolved. Then boil rapidly for 1-2 minutes. Remove from heat and stir in rose water. Keep aside.

Scrape malai off sides of kadhai. Put a thin layer in the dish. Brush some sugar syrup on top and sprinkle with some sliced pistachio nuts. Add another layer of malai, sugar syrup and pistachio nuts and continue till all the malai is used up. (Do not scrape the brown part at the bottom of the kadhai).

Put a piece of greaseproof paper or foil on top of the khurchan and press gently to level the top.

Chill before serving.

KULFI

Makes: 12-15

This frozen milk dessert was developed in Delhi by the Mughals. They brought ice to Delhi from a mountain near Kasauli called Choori Chandni ka Dhar which is perennially covered with snow. Abu'L Fazl tells us that saltpetre for cooling was introduced to India by Akbar.

The method of making kulfi has remained unchanged to the present day. Thickened milk is put into special conical moulds and frozen by putting these in a large pot filled with a mixture of ice and salt, which is shaken gently till the kulfi freezes. The moulds can be of metal, but the traditional earthenware moulds give a lovely flavour to the kulfi.

A baraf ki handi—a pot full of kulfi is a very special gift to send someone.

The festival of teej and sindhara which falls sometime in August is meant for girls—teej for daughters and sindhara for daughters-in-law. A married girl goes to her parent's house a day or so before the festival and her whole family is invited to celebrate sindhara. Her in-laws send clothes, jewellery, toys, a swing, sweets and as a special sign of affection, a baraf ki handi and a khomcha of chaat. (A chaat vendor with his paraphernalia for making chaat.) The swing is put up, the family oohs and aahs, everybody eats the chaat and kulfi and the girl's proud mother beams at how much her daughter is loved by her in-laws!

With a refrigerator, kulfi can be made at home without the pot and the ice.

2 litres full cream milk
150 gm (¾ cup) sugar
50 gm (approx. 40) almonds, blanched and ground
Few drops kewra essence
Metal kulfi moulds, washed and dried

Put milk into a large pan and bring to boil. Reduce heat and
continue to cook, stirring from time to time till milk has reduced
to a little less than half original volume. This will take 30-40
minutes. Remove from heat, add sugar and stir to dissolve. Stir in
almonds and essence. Cool mixture, then pour into kulfi moulds
leaving one inch space at the top for kulfi to expand. Cover firmly
with lids and put in freezer for 8-10 hours till frozen.

To serve, roll mould in your hands, run a sharp knife around
inside edge and unmould onto a plate.

MANGO KULFI

Makes: 15-18

Make as in previous recipe but omit the almonds and essence. Cool milk and sugar mixture and stir in 300 ml pureed mango. If the mango is very sweet you may need to reduce the quantity of sugar.

A cheaper alternative to kulfi is the baraf ka gola or water ice. To make these a little sherbet (khas, rose or sandalwood) is used to sweeten, flavour and colour crushed ice. This is then compacted around a stick. These green, pink and yellow confections can be seen in the markets of the old city and are very popular with children.

DAULAT KI CHAAT
Milk Puff

Makes: 40-50 small bowls

This divine confection can only be made in winter and is best eaten the day it is made. It is not really a dessert as it can be had at any time. As children, Heaven was a fridge full of daulat ki chaat and one could eat it all day through.

2 litres full cream milk, unboiled
500 gm (2¼ cups) cream
1 heaped tsp cream of tartar
200 gm (1 cup) caster sugar
1 tsp rose water
25 gm (2 tbsp) pistachio nuts, finely sliced

Combine milk, cream and cream of tartar in a large bowl and refrigerate overnight.

Next morning stir in 4 tsp caster sugar and rose water and whisk mixture using a rotary or electric beater at high speed. Using a tea strainer collect the foam that forms and transfer to a large thali or tray. Keep thali tilted so that foam stays on one side; some milk will collect on the lower side. When thali is fairly full, spoon foam into clay saucers or teacups, sprinkling a little caster sugar between layers and on top. (The foam will condense a little during this operation. What looks like four bowlfuls in the thali will yield only two bowls.)

Pour milk collected in thali back into bowl and continue beating and collecting foam till all the milk is used up. The whole process will take 2-2½ hours.

Sprinkle sliced pistachio nuts on top of each bowl of foam and refrigerate till serving time.

The Daulat ki Chaat can also be layered in 2-3 large bowls but it loses some of its fluffiness and becomes dense.

SOOJI KA HALVA
Semolina Halva

Serves: 10-12

All halvas are best made in a kadhai. Pure ghee adds greatly to the flavour.

> 6 green cardamoms
> 1 litre water
> 500 gm (2½ cups) sugar
> 250 gm (1¼ cup) ghee (no substitute)
> 250 gm (1⅓ cup) semolina
> 25 gm (2 tbsp) sultanas (kishmish)
> 25 gm (approx. 20) almonds, sliced

Remove seeds from cardamoms, grind and keep aside. Put cardamom skins, water and sugar into pan and stir over low heat till sugar dissolves. Keep aside.

Heat ghee in a kadhai or wok, add semolina, cook and stir over moderate heat till pale gold—do not let it become too brown. Stir in sultanas and almonds and cook for 1-2 minutes.

Carefully strain sugar syrup into semolina. Stir and cook for 5 minutes or so till liquid is absorbed and mixture is paste-like. Stir in powdered cardamom seeds.

Serve hot.

GAAJAR KA HALVA
Carrot Halva

Serves: 8-10

A friend who was posted in China had impressed upon her Chinese cook the importance of garnishing all Indian dishes with chopped coriander. At one party he proudly brought in the gaajar ka halva duly sprinkled with fresh coriander!

1 kg red 'desi' carrots
2 litres milk
200 gm (1 cup) sugar
250 gm (1¼ cups) ghee (no substitute)
Seeds of 8 green cardamoms, powdered
50 gm (4 tbsp) sultanas (kishmish)
50 gm (⅓ cup) almonds, blanched and sliced

Wash and scrape carrots, and grate into fine, long shreds. Put into a large pan, cover and cook over medium heat without adding any water for 10-15 minutes.

Add milk and cook uncovered stirring from time to time till mixture is dry. This will take about one hour or more. Add sugar and ghee and continue to stir and cook till sugar dissolves and halva is a rich orange colour. It is important to keep scraping the bottom of the pan to prevent halva from burning. Stir in cardamom, sultanas and almonds. Serve warm

This halva keeps very well in the refrigerator for several days and becomes tastier each time it is re-heated. You can make a lighter version of this very rich halva by reducing the milk to one litre and the ghee to 150 gms.

MUNG DAL HALVA
Husked Green Bean Halva

Serves: 10-12

180 gm (1 cup) husked green beans (dhuli mung ki dal)
12 green cardamoms
350 gm (1½ cups) sugar
200 gm (1 cup) ghee (no substitute)
1 tsp gram flour
120 ml milk
50 gm (⅓ cup) almonds, sliced
50 gm (4 tbsp) sultanas

Soak dal in water for 8-10 hours. Drain and grind to a fine paste.

Peel cardamoms, powder seeds and keep aside. Put skins into a pan with sugar and pour in 2 cups water. Stir over moderate heat till sugar is dissolved, then simmer for 2 minutes. Remove from fire and keep aside.

Melt ghee in a kadhai or wok and fry gram flour till lightly coloured. (This prevents dal from sticking to the bottom of the kadhai.) Remove from heat and add dal paste.

Return to medium heat and cook, stirring constantly. Do not worry if the mixture seems to become one mass at first; keep stirring and add milk a little at a time, it will soon separate into granules. Stir and cook till golden—when it is done the fat will begin to separate.

Stir in almonds and sultanas and cook for 1-2 minutes.

Strain reserved sugar syrup into mixture and continue to cook and stir till water is absorbed and consistency is paste-like. Add reserved powdered cardamoms and serve hot.

ANDE KA HALVA
Egg Halva

Serves: 8-10

A recipe from the *Pukht-o-Paaz*.

24 egg-yolks
250 gm (1¼ cups) sugar
250 gm (1¼ cups) ghee (no substitute)
6 cloves, powdered
Seeds of 6 green cardamoms, powdered
Pinch saffron
2-3 drops kewra essence
25 gm (approx. 20) almonds, sliced
25 gm (2 tbsp) pistachio nuts, sliced

Beat egg-yolks and sugar together thoroughly till pale and frothy.

Heat ghee in a kadhai or wok just till melted. Remove from heat and beat in yolk mixture. Return to very low heat and cook, stirring constantly, till mixture thickens. Watch very carefully and do not allow mixture to become grainy or ghee to separate. The halva should be smooth and glossy.

Remove from fire and immediately turn out into a bowl, as the heat in the pan will continue to cook the eggs and spoil the halva. Stir in cloves, cardamom, saffron dissolved in 2-3 tsp hot water and kewra essence.

Sprinkle nuts on top. Cool and serve.

GUDAMBA
Green Mango Halva

Serves: 6-8

A recipe from the *Pukht-o-Paaz.*

10 (approx. 1 kg) unripe mangoes
100 gm (⅔ cup) semolina
120 gm (⅔ cup) ghee (no substitute)
250 gm (1¼ cups) sugar
6 cloves
6 green cardamoms

Choose mangoes that are not too sour. Peel mangoes and cut off flesh with a sharp knife.

Discard seeds and put flesh into a pan. Cover with water and cook on moderate heat till tender. Drain and keep aside.

Roast semolina on a griddle till lightly coloured.

Put sugar into a pan with 500 ml water and stir over moderate heat till dissolved. Simmer for 2-3 minutes.

Stir roasted semolina into sugar syrup and keep aside.

Heat half the ghee in a kadhai or wok, add mango pulp, stir and cook for 3-5 minutes. Pour in semolina and sugar mixture, cook and stir till mixture begins to boil. Remove from heat.

Heat remaining ghee and fry cloves and cardamoms for 2-3 minutes. Pour into halva and mix. Serve hot.

Note: This halva has a fairly thin consistency.

BESAN KE LADDOO
Gram Flour Laddoos

Makes: 25-30

200 gm (1 cup) ghee (no substitute)
250 gm (2 cups) gram flour (besan)
125 gm (⅔ cup) caster sugar
25 gm (approx. 20) almonds, finely sliced

Heat ghee in a kadhai or wok. Add gram flour and cook on low heat for 10-15 minutes till lightly coloured. Do not allow mixture to get too brown.

Remove from heat, stir in sugar and almonds. When mixture is cool enough to handle, form into walnut sized balls. Cool completely and store till required.

PISTE KI LAUZ
Pistachio Sweet

Serves: 4-5

This very special Delhi sweet is neither a barfi nor a toffee, but something far superior. Buy very fresh unsalted pistachio nuts in the shell for this sweet. 500 gms nuts in the shell should yield 250 gms when shelled.

250 gm shelled, unsalted pistachio nuts
200 gm (1 cup) sugar
50 ml water
Silver leaf (varak)

Put pistachio into a bowl. Pour in enough boiling water to cover. Leave for 3-5 minutes, drain, remove skins and grind coarsely.

Put sugar and 50 ml water into a pan and stir over gentle heat till sugar dissolves. Simmer for 2-3 minutes. Add ground pistachio nuts and cook, stirring constantly, till mixture leaves sides of pan.

Pour into a greased plate and level the top. Cool and decorate with silver leaf. Cut into squares and serve.

BADAAM KI LAUZ
Almond Sweet

This is made in the same way as Piste ki Lauz using almonds instead of pistachio nuts.

PARVAL KI MITHAI
Wax Gourd Sweet

Serves: 12-15

1 kg wax gourd (parval)
½ kg (2½ cups) sugar
2½ litres milk
Juice of 2 limes
150 gm (¾ cup) caster sugar
1 tsp rose water
50 gm (⅓ cup) almonds
50 gm (4 tbsp) pistachio nuts
Seeds of 8 green cardamoms, powdered
2 tbsp crushed sugar candy (misri)
½ tsp powdered saffron (optional)

Choose tender, even sized wax gourd. Peel and put into a large pan. Cover with water bring to boil, then simmer for 10 minutes.

Drain and cool. Make a slit along length of each wax gourd. Remove and discard seeds and pulp.

Put sugar in a pan with 500 ml water and stir over gentle heat till sugar dissolves. Boil rapidly for 2-3 minutes. Remove from heat and stir in rose water. Put hollowed wax gourd into sugar syrup and leave aside for 3-4 hours. They will become pale green and translucent.

Put milk into a large pan and bring to boil. Pour in lime juice and stir till it curdles.

Remove from heat and stir till all the milk has curdled and water has separated. Tie in muslin and put under a weight for 1½-2 hours.

Put almonds and pistachio nuts into a small pan and cover

with water. Bring to boil and simmer for 5 minutes. Drain, remove skins and chop nuts finely.

Untie cottage cheese and grind to a paste. Mix in sugar candy, almonds, pistachios and powdered cardamom.

Drain wax gourds from sugar syrup. (Discard syrup). Fill with cottage cheese mixture and sprinkle a little powdered saffron on top.

Chill till ready to serve.

Snacks and Accompaniments

MATHRI
Semolina and Flour Savoury

Makes: 20-25

At one time every Mathur household had a stock of mathris. These along with besan ke laddoo were meant to be eaten at 'nashta'—a term covering both breakfast and evening tea.

Mathris make an excellent anytime snack and are delicious with pickle, or with left over meat or vegetables.

> 100 gm (scant 1 cup) flour
> 300 gm (2 cups) semolina
> ½ tsp thyme seeds (ajwain)
> ½ tsp salt
> 60 gm (4 tbsp) ghee + 500 gm (2½ cups) for frying

Mix together flour, semolina, thyme and salt. Rub in 4 tbsp ghee. Add enough water to make a fairly stiff dough.

Pinch off walnut sized pieces of dough and roll out to ⅛ inch thickness. Prick all over with a fork to prevent mathris from puffing.

Heat 500 gms ghee in a kadhai or deep frying pan till smoking, reduce heat and fry mathris till lightly coloured.

NAGORI POORI
Semolina Savoury

Makes: 20-25

These are called pooris, but are more akin to mathris. An old
family cure for a cold was to have a nagori with dry kofta!

500 gm (3 heaped cups) semolina
½ tsp thyme seeds (ajwain)
½ tsp salt
5 tbsp ghee + 500 gm (2½ cups) for frying

Mix together semolina, thyme and salt. Rub in 5 tbsp ghee. Add
enough water to make a stiff dough.

Pinch off walnut sized pieces of dough and roll out to ⅛ inch
thickness. Do not prick.

Heat ghee in a kadhai or deep frying pan till smoking, reduce
heat and fry nagori till puffed up and lightly coloured.

PAPRI
Gram Flour Savouries

Makes: 25-30

These gram flour savouries (not to be confused with papri chaat) are traditionally made in Mathur homes at Holi and Diwali. Papri making is a communal activity and all the ladies of the family get together a few days before the festival to make the dough, roll out and fry the papris. They must be rolled out as thinly as possible and the larger you make them the greater is the skill required in the rolling and frying process.

In the first year of a girl's marriage, her mother sends papris (along with other goodies) to her in-law's home. All her aunts get into the act and decorate the papris with frills and designs made with contrasting white flour dough. These must be fried just so; the papri being yellow and the design remaining white.

Today not many people find the time to make papris, let alone the frills and furbelows!

A new bride remains 'new' for the entire first year of marriage. All the festivals in that year are referred to as the couple's first Holi or first Diwali and are more special than subsequent Holis and Diwalis.

Holi is a festival of fun and games. A new bride on her first Holi has to lock her parents-in-law together in a room and extract a promise of a gift before releasing them! This may be easily accomplished today, but in the large joint families of earlier times it was no mean task.

250 gm (2 cups) gram flour (besan)
1 tsp salt
Pinch cream of tartar
½ tsp powdered red chillies
Pinch powdered asafoetida
5-6 fenugreek leaves, finely chopped
½-¾ cup water
A little flour for dusting
500 ml mustard oil for frying

Mix all dry ingredients and chopped fenugreek together. Add water a little at a time to make a very stiff dough. Take 2 tbsp mustard oil in a small bowl. Gradually knead this into dough. (The dough is very stiff and is difficult to knead with the hands—you will have to pound it with a grinding stone or rolling pin).

With oiled hands roll dough into a long rope about one inch in diameter. Cut off one inch pieces of dough.

Using oiled hands flatten each into a circle. Dust work surface with flour and roll out papris as thinly as possible. They should be 5-6 inches in diameter.

Heat oil in a large kadhai or wok till smoking, reduce heat and fry papris till cooked through and crisp. Do not allow papri to become too dark—the finished product should be pale gold.

Cool and store carefully in an airtight container.

GOOJA
Sweet Turnovers

Makes: 25

These pastry turnovers are filled with a mixture of sweetened milk solids (khoya) and nuts. They are traditionally made at Diwali and Holi.

250 gm (2 cups) plain flour (maida)
75 gm (5 tbsp) ghee
2-3 tbsp cold water
250 gm khoya (dried unsweetened condensed milk)
200 gm (1 cup) sugar
25 gm (approx. 20) almonds, blanched and sliced
25 gm (2 tbsp) sultanas (kishmish)
25 gm (3 tbsp) chironji
Seeds of 5 green cardamoms, powdered
500 gm (2½ cups) ghee for frying

Rub ghee into flour. Add enough cold water to make a soft, not sticky dough. Knead till smooth, cover with a damp cloth and keep aside.

Crumble khoya, put into a kadhai or deep frying pan and roast over gentle heat till light brown. Cool. Mix in sugar, almonds, sultanas, chironji and cardamom.

Pinch off a small piece of dough and roll out into a circle about 4 inches in diameter. (You can use a saucer as a guide).

Put 2 tsp khoya mixture onto half the circle, leaving the edge clear. Moisten edge with water and fold other half of dough over to encase filling. Seal edges and crimp with fingers to form a fluted edge. Make remaining goojas in the same way.

Heat ghee in a kadhai and fry goojas a few at a time till golden.

Cool completely and store in an airtight container.

MEVA KE GOOJE
Nut-filled Turnovers

Makes: 30-35

250 gm (2 cups) plain flour
75 gm (5 tbsp) ghee
2-3 tbsp cold water
50 gm (⅓ cup) almonds, blanched
50 gm (4 tbsp) pistachio nuts, blanched
25 gm (2 tbsp) chironji
2 tsp marsh melon seeds
25 gm (2 tbsp) sultanas
2 tsp sugar
500 gm (2½ cups) ghee for frying

Rub ghee into flour and mix in enough cold water to make a soft, not sticky dough. Knead for a few minutes, cover with a damp cloth and keep aside.

Finely chop almonds and pistachio. Lightly roast chironji and melon seeds on griddle for 2-3 minutes. Mix with nuts, sultanas and sugar.

Roll pastry into 3 inch circles and fill with a teaspoon of nut mixture.

Moisten edges, seal and crimp as described in previous recipe.

Heat ghee in a kadhai or wok and fry goojas till golden. Cool completely and store in an airtight container.

KEOKA
Sugared Seeds

Keoka is the collective name for a variety of sugared seeds which are given to a nursing mother. Pure ghee is used as it is meant to be 'strengthening'. Keoka is also made at the festival of Janam Ashtmi as this celebrates the birth of Lord Krishna.

Powdered khandsari (boora) used in these recipes is available at most grocers. You can use caster sugar but boora gives better results.

MAKHANE
Sugared Lotus Seeds

100 gm lotus seeds
4-5 level tbsp pure ghee
4-5 heaped tbsp boora or castor sugar

Remove any hard black bits on lotus seeds. Dry roast in a kadhai or wok for 2-3 minutes. Remove and keep aside.

Heat ghee in kadhai, stir in lotus seeds and cook till ghee is absorbed. Add boora, flick in a little water with your fingers and stir to coat lotus seeds with sugar. Work quickly and do not allow sugar to caramelise. Turn out onto a plate. Cool and store in an airtight container

BEEJ
Sugared Marsh Melon Seeds

100 gm marsh melon seeds
3-4 heaped tbsp boora or castor sugar

Dry roast melon seeds in a kadhai or wok for 1-2 minutes. Add boora, flick in a little water with your fingers and stir till seeds are coated with sugar. Turn out onto a plate. Cool and store in an airtight container.

CHIRONJI
Sugared Chironji

100 gm chironji
4 heaped tbsp boora or castor sugar

This is made exactly like the melon seeds.

GARI
Sugared Copra

1 dry coconut (copra), grated
6-8 heaped tbsp boora

Dry roast coconut in a kadhai or wok for 2-3 minutes. Add boora
and a handful of water. Stir till coconut is coated with sugar. Turn
out onto a plate and press down gently. Cut into diamonds and
serve.

GOND
Sugared Edible Gum

Gond (edible gum) is supposed to be very good for the back. It is
best had when freshly made.

100 gm gond (choose gond that is white rather than brownish)
200 gm (1 cup) ghee
4-5 heaped tbsp boora or castor sugar

Heat ghee in a kadhai or wok and fry gond till it is puffed up and
opaque. Drain and toss in boora to coat. Serve as soon as it is cool.

KEEME KA SAMOSA
Mutton Samosa

Makes: 40-44

Pastry:

250 gm (2 cups) flour
Pinch of salt
5 level tbsp ghee (no substitute)
5-6 tbsp water

Filling:

500 gm finely minced mutton
3 tbsp ghee
2 medium onions, finely chopped
8 cloves garlic, ground
½ inch piece ginger, finely chopped
½ tsp turmeric powder
1 tsp powdered coriander seeds
4 tbsp curd
1½ tsp salt
2 tbsp finely chopped fresh coriander
500 gm (2½ cups) ghee for frying

Pastry: Sieve flour and salt together and rub in ghee. Add enough water to make a stiff dough and knead till smooth. Cover with a damp cloth and keep aside.

Filling: Heat 3 tbsp ghee and fry onions till golden. Add garlic, ginger, turmeric and coriander powder, stir and cook, adding curd a little at a time. Add salt and mince and cook till mince is evenly browned. Pour in 250 ml water, cover and cook for 30-45 minutes till mince is tender and completely dry. Stir in chopped fresh coriander. Cool completely before using.

Samosas: Pinch off small pieces of dough and roll out thinly into circles. Cut each circle in half.

Moisten half the cut edge with water and fold over other half to make a cone shape. Press firmly to seal. Hold open cone in one hand and fill with 2-3 tsp mince. Moisten top edge and seal to enclose filling. Crimp edges.

Heat ghee in a kadhai or wok and fry samosas till golden on all sides.

SABUT MATAR
Peas in the Pod

Serves: 4-5

Choose fresh green peas with thick skins for this tea-time snack.
The peas are cooked in their skins and are eaten by putting a whole
pod in your mouth and sucking out the peas and tender inner skin
with your teeth.

500 gm unshelled green peas
2 tbsp ghee
Pinch asafoetida
½ tsp cumin seeds
1-2 tsp salt
3 tsp powdered green mango (amchur)
1 tsp garam masala powder

Wash peas and discard any discoloured pods.

Heat ghee in a large kadhai or wok. Add asafoetida and cumin
and fry for one minute. Add whole peas, salt, powdered green
mango and garam masala and mix together. Reduce heat, cover
and cook, stirring occasionally, for 15-20 minutes till peas are
tender. Adjust seasoning to taste and serve.

CHAAT KA MASALA

Makes: ⅓ cup

2 tsp cumin seeds
1 tsp black perppercorn
1 whole dried red chilli
1 tsp powdered dried ginger
2 tsp black salt (kala namak)
3 tsp powdered dried green mango (amchur)
1 tsp salt
Pinch asafoetida

Roast cumin seeds and peppercorns on a griddle.

Grind with red chilli and mix in remaining ingredients. Bottle and keep till required.

This masala is used to garnish a variety of 'chaat' snacks.

PAPRI CHAAT
Savoury Biscuits with Curd

Serves: 6-8

The word chaat means 'to lick'. These spicy snacks are traditionally served in dried leaf platters, which were often actually licked clean! If it rains at a wedding it is said that the bride or groom must have licked their chaat platters as children.

Papri:

250 gm (1½ cups) flour
½ tsp salt
½ tsp cumin seeds

6-8 tbsp cold water
2 tbsp ghee, melted
500 gm ghee for frying

Dahi:

500 gm (2½ cups) curd
1½ tsp salt
2-3 tsp roasted, powdered cumin seed
1 tsp powdered red chilli
Meethi sonth chutney (see recipe pg. 260)

Papri: Sieve flour and salt together. Add cumin seeds and enough cold water to make a stiff dough. Knead thoroughly, adding melted ghee into dough. Roll out thinly and cut out circles 1½ inches in diameter. Prick papris with a fork.

Heat ghee in a kadhai or wok and fry papris a few at a time till golden. Drain and keep aside.

Dahi: Whip curd and add salt and cumin to taste. Keep aside.

Just before serving, arrange papris in a platter, pour seasoned curd and meethi sonth on top. Sprinkle with powdered cumin, red chillies and chaat masala.

KALMI BARÉ
Bengal Gram Fritters

Serves: 6-8

1 cup Bengal Gram (chana dal)
¼ cup husked black gram (dhuli urad ki dal)
1 tsp salt
1 rounded tsp whole black peppercorn
2 tsp coriander seeds, roughly crushed
1-2 green chillies, finely chopped
2 tbsp chopped fresh coriander
500 gm ghee for frying
Garam masala or chaat masala to sprinkle

Wash and soak dals together in plenty of water for 8-10 hours. Drain and grind to a fine paste. Mix in remaining ingredients except ghee and beat thoroughly till light and fluffy.

Heat ghee in a kadhai or wok till smoking. Drop in rounded tablespoonfuls of paste to make large pakoras. When bubbles appear on the surface, turn and fry other side till pale gold. Drain and cool. Cut each pakora crosswise into ¼ inch slices. (Do not worry if the centre appears uncooked.) Reheat ghee and fry slices till deep gold and crisp.

Sprinkle with garam or chaat masala and serve with green chutney.

DAHI KI GUJIYA

Stuffed Black Gram Fritters in Curd

Makes: 10-12

Gujia:

250 gm (1¼ cups) husked black beans (dhuli urad ki dal)
½ tsp bicarbonate of soda (meetha soda)
Pinch asafoetida
2 inch piece ginger, finely chopped
1-2 green chillies, finely chopped
2 tsp finely chopped mint leaves
25 gm (2 tbsp) sultanas (kishmish)
500 gm (2½ cups) ghee for frying

Dahi:

500 gm (4 cups) curd
2 tsp cumin seeds, roasted and ground
¼ tsp powdered red chilli
1 tsp salt

Garnish:

Roasted, powdered cumin seeds
Powdered red chilli

Gujia: Soak dal in cold water for 8-10 hours. Drain and grind to a fine paste. Mix in soda and asafoetida and whip mixture till fluffy.

Mix together ginger, chillies, mint and sultanas and keep aside.

Heat ghee in a kadhai or wok.

Stretch a moistened piece of muslin over rim of a katori or glass. Using wet hands make small balls of mixture and flatten lightly on the muslin. Put a small amount of ginger mixture in the centre and fold over to make a semi-circle, using the muslin to aid you. Gently press edges to enclose filling.

Test if ghee is hot enough by putting a small amount of dal paste into kadhai—it should float to the surface almost immediately.

Using a wet knife slide gujiya carefully into hot ghee and fry till pale gold. Make the rest in the same way.

Put fried gujiyas into a bowl of warm, salted water and leave for 10 minutes.

Dahi: Whip curd and mix in cumin, chilli and salt.

Gently squeeze gujiyas with your palms to extract excess water and arrange in a shallow dish. Pour over seasoned curd to cover gujiyas.

Garnish with powdered cumin and red chillies.

Serve chilled.

DAHI BARA
Black Gram Fritters in Curd

These are made in the same way as the gujiya. Omit the filling and make slightly smaller circles of dal paste on the wet cloth. Fry, soak and add to curd as above.

DAHI KI PAKORI
Black Gram Balls in Curd

The same dal paste can be used for dahi ki pakoris. Put teaspoonfuls of paste into hot ghee and fry till golden. Soak in warm salted water for 10-15 minutes, squeeze and put into seasoned curd.

These pakoris can also be added to papri chaat.

KELE KE DAHI BARÉ
Green Banana Fritters in Curd

Serves: 4-6

6 green cooking bananas
½ tsp salt
Pinch pepper
1-2 green chillies, finely cut
2 tsp chopped fresh coriander
250 gm (1¼ cups) ghee for frying
500 gm (4 cups) curd
1 tsp salt
½ tsp cumin seeds, roasted and ground
½ tsp sugar
Pinch pepper

Bring a large pan of water to boil. Put in whole bananas and cook for 10-15 minutes. Drain and cool slightly, then peel. Mash bananas and mix in next 4 ingredients.

Take a little mixture and form into a ball with your hands. Flatten into small circles with the palms. You will get 12-14 baras.

Heat ghee in a kadhai or deep frying pan and fry baras till golden. Keep aside.

Whip curd and stir in remaining ingredients.

Arrange banana baras in a shallow dish and pour seasoned curd on top to cover baras completely. Chill till ready to serve.

GOLGAPPA
Puffed Biscuits with Spiced Water

Makes: 50

½ cup wholewheat flour (atta)
½ cup semolina
2 tbsp ghee
2-3 tbsp water
500 gm ghee for frying
Boiled chickpeas and chopped boiled potatoes to serve
Jal zeera (see following recipe)

Mix together flour and semolina. Rub in ghee and mix to a stiff dough with water. Cover with a damp cloth and leave for 30 minutes. Pinch off marble sized pieces of dough and roll thinly into 1½ inch circles. Heat ghee in a kadhai or wok till smoking and fry golgappas till puffed up and golden. (If golgappas brown too quickly, reduce heat.)

To serve make a hole in the top crust of golgappa, put in some potato and chickpeas, dip in jal zeera to fill and eat immediately.

JAL ZEERA
Spiced Water to Serve with Golgappa

Serves: 6-8

12 dried kachri
12 slices dried mango (sabut amchur)
1 tsp powdered dried ginger (sonth)
12 whole dried red chillies
1 rounded tsp whole black peppercorn
4 tsp cumin seeds, lightly roasted
4 tsp black salt (kala namak)
¼ tsp asafoetida
1½ tsp salt

Mix all ingredients together in a glass or stainless steel bowl. Pour in 4 cups hot water, cover and leave to soak for 8-10 hours or overnight. Strain water and adjust seasoning to taste. Chill and serve.

Traditionally jal zeera was served in an earthenware pot which had been smoked with asafoetida. To do this heat a small piece of coal till red hot and put into a small bowl. Add a pea-sized piece of asafoetida and immediately invert an earthenware pot over the bowl. Leave for 10 minutes. Pour in jal zeera and let it stand for one hour before serving.

Note: This makes a cooling drink by itself.

ALU KE KULLE
Potato Cups

Makes: 12

For Alu ke Kulle potatoes are roasted in charcoal embers, hollowed and filled with a mixture of masalas, lime juice and boiled gram. For the genuine kulla you have to go to Nai Sarak and get it from the shop of Sultan, whose combination of masalas is a family secret. However, a reasonable imitation can be made at home.

12 medium sized potatoes
1 tsp salt
1 tsp chaat masala
1-2 green chillies, finely chopped
2 tsp finely chopped fresh coriander
Juice of 2 limes

Cook potatoes in plenty of boiling salted water for 30-40 minutes till done.

Peel when cool enough to handle.

Cut a thin slice off top of each potato and keep aside. Using a teaspoon, scrape out some potato from centre, making a depression. Fill with a pinch of salt, chaat masala, green chilli and coriander. Drizzle in a little lime juice, replace top and serve immediately.

BURRANI

Aubergine Salad to Accompany
Pulao

1 large aubergine (approx. 500 gm)
60 gm (4 tbsp) ghee
1 medium onion, sliced
1 kg (8 cups) curd
1 tsp salt
½ tsp pepper
Pinch powdered red chilli
6 cloves garlic, ground

Peel aubergine and slice finely.

Heat ghee and fry aubergine till lightly coloured. Drain and keep aside. In the same ghee fry onion till pale gold. Drain.

Whip curd and pass through a sieve. Stir in aubergine, onion, salt, pepper and chilli. Put the ground garlic in a piece of muslin and squeeze juice into curd mixture. Stir and chill till ready to serve.

KHATTE KACHALU
Sour Kachalu to Accompany Rich Fried Food

Kachalu is a vegetable that looks like a potato, and has a texture similar to colocasia.

½ kg kachalu
4 tsp powdered, dried green mango (amchur)
1 tsp powdered red chilli
1 tsp black salt (kala namak)
1 tsp salt
1 tsp cumin seeds
Pinch asafoetida
1 tsp garam masala powder
2 inch piece ginger, cut into fine strands
1-2 green chillies, finely chopped
Juice of 2 limes

Cut kachalu in half and cook in boiling water till just tender. Drain and cool slightly. Peel kachalu and cut into slices. Keep aside.

Grind together green mango, red chilli, black salt, salt, cumin seeds and asafoetida with 3-4 tsp water. Mix in garam masala, ginger, green chillies and lime juice. Add a little more water if necessary—the masala should be paste-like and not too thin.

Stir in kachalu and chill till ready to serve.

GOTA
Betel Nut Mixture

This is a mixture of coconut, aniseed and betelnut that is served at the end of a meal along with or instead of paan. Before a wedding large quantities of gota are made and kept, and is eaten before, after and even between meals!

2 dry coconuts
200 gm aniseed (saunf), lightly roasted
200 gm husked coriander seeds (dhania dana)
100 gm sweet betelnut (meethi supari)

Cut each coconut in half and grate. Mix in remaining ingredients. Store in an airtight container.

This keeps for 3-4 weeks.

Chutneys and Pickles

No Indian meal is complete without pickles and chutneys. In less busy times pickle making was serious business and carried on throughout the year depending upon the fruit and vegetables in season. Since the pickle was meant to last from one season to the next, huge quantities were made and one or two days were set aside for this task. Pickles are temperamental and all utensils used have to be completely clean. At one time unclean (i.e. menstruating) women were not allowed to touch the jars of pickle for fear of contamination! Today a wide variety of commercial pickles are available in the market but there is a certain satisfaction in making your own.

HARI CHUTNEY
Mint and Coriander Chutney

Makes: ¾ cup

2 handfuls fresh mint leaves
2 handfuls fresh coriander (leaves and tender stems only)
2 green chillies, chopped
1 tsp salt
1 tsp sugar
2 tsp powdered dried green mango (amchur) or juice of 2 limes

Grind all ingredients together. This is best made on a grinding stone.

If using an electric grinder, use lime juice instead of dried green mango.

This chutney stays for 3-4 days in the refrigerator.

PYAZ KA LACHCHA
Onion Relish

Makes: 1 cup

In the days of the joint family, one of the tests of a new bride's culinary competence was how finely she could slice onions for lachcha. I'm afraid I failed to meet the high standard set by my grandmother and therefore never tried it in my in-law's home!

2 large onions
2 tsp chopped fresh coriander
½ tsp salt
1-2 green chillies, finely chopped
Juice of 1 large or 2 small limes

Cut onions in half from root to tip; then cut crosswise as finely as possible. (A good hausfrau cuts the onions into almost threadlike shreds—this can take her practically the whole morning, leaving very little time for any other work!)

Soak sliced onions in cold water for 30 minutes.

Drain and mix in remaining ingredients.

This is best served freshly made.

SONTH KI CHUTNEY
Dried Ginger Chutney

Makes: 1 cup

For best results, use a grinding stone for this chutney.

½ inch piece dried ginger
4 tbsp cumin seeds
15-20 black peppercorns
5 dried red chillies
1 dried kachri
10-12 pieces dried green mango (sabut amchur)
¼ tsp black salt (kala namak)
Pinch asafoetida
1 tsp salt

Put all ingredients except asafoetida and salt in a small bowl, cover with cold water and soak for one hour.

Drain and reserve water. Grind spices to a fine paste using a little of the soaking water. Add asafoetida and salt in the final stages of grinding.

This chutney will keep in the refrigerator for one week.

MEETHI SONTH
Sweet and Sour Tamarind Chutney

Makes: 2 cups

150 gm tamarind
3-4 tbsp jaggery (gur)
1 tsp dry ginger, powdered
1 tsp roasted, powdered cumin seeds
2 tsp salt
½ tsp powdered red chilli

Soak tamarind in 750 ml boiled water for 1-2 hours. Pass through a sieve, squeezing out all the pulp.

Mix in remaining ingredients and stir to dissolve jaggery. Adjust seasoning to taste and add a little more water if chutney is too thick. Chill till ready to serve.

SAUNF KI CHUTNEY
Aniseed Chutney

Makes: ½ cup

This chutney is served with bervin (stuffed poori) and potatoes.

3 tsp aniseed (saunf), roughly crushed
2 tsp coriander seeds, roughly crushed
1 tsp salt
½ tsp powdered red chilli
½ tsp turmeric powder
2 tsp fenugreek seeds (methi dana)
3-4 dried kachri, ground
4 tsp coarsely powdered dried green mango (amchur)
1 tbsp cooking oil
½ tsp cumin seeds
Pinch asafoetida

Soak first 8 ingredients in one cup water for 3-4 hours.

Heat oil in a small pan. Add cumin and asafoetida and fry for half a minute. Add soaked ingredients along with water. Cook on medium heat for 10-15 minutes, stirring occasionally, till chutney is thick and fenugreek seeds are soft. Cool and serve.

This chutney keeps in the refrigerator for 3-4 days.

AAM KI MEETHI CHUTNEY
Sweet Mango Chutney

5 kg unripe mangoes, peeled and grated
200 gm fresh ginger, grated
100 gm garlic, peeled and chopped
150 gm salt
60 gm black salt (kala nakak)
Seeds of 100 gm black cardamoms, coarsely pounded
50 gm black peppercorn
60 gm aniseed, lightly roasted and coarsely ground
20 gm powdered red chilli
3 kg sugar
1½ bottles malt vinegar

Mix mangoes, ginger, garlic, salt and all the spices together in a large pan and leave for 10 minutes, till some liquid collects in the pan.

Add sugar and vinegar and cook on moderate heat till mixture comes to the boil. Reduce heat and simmer for 10-15 minutes till mixture thickens. Stir carefully from time to time; the strands of grated mango should not break.

Pour into sterilized jars, cover and store.

This chutney should last for one year.

NEEBU KA ACHAAR
Lime Pickle

10 kg even sized limes
250 gm black peppercorn
125 gm cumin seeds
60 gm black cardamom seeds
60 gm thyme seeds (ajwain)
10 gm cloves
10 gm cinnamon
125 gm dried ginger (soonth)
2 nutmegs
½ tsp mace flakes
25 gm peepul (available at most grocer's)
1½ kg rock salt (lahori namak), ground

Wash and dry limes.

Grind all spices and mix with salt.

Make two right-angled cuts across limes almost all the way down to stalk end. Fill with ground masala.

Put limes into a jar and cover tightly. Place jar in the sun for one month.

This pickle will last for one year.

When this pickle is left long enough it becomes completely dry. The dry pickle can be ground and used as a remedy for nausea.

Note: If rock salt is not available, use ordinary salt.

PYAZ LAHSAN KA ACHAAR
Onion and Garlic Pickle

Pinch asafoetida + 2 tsp sesame oil
1 kg sesame oil
2 tbsp fenugreek seeds
4 tbsp onion seeds
3 tbsp cumin seeds
60 gm (6 tbsp) jaggery (gur)
50 ml (3½ tbsp) malt vinegar
Seeds of 10 green cardamoms, ground
125 gm fresh ginger, grated
125 gm whole dried red chillies, ground
125 gm (½ cup) salt
125 gm (¾ cup) mustard seeds (rai), ground
250 gm garlic, peeled
125 gm button onions, peeled
1 kg peeled and grated raw mangoes

Put asafoetida and 2 tsp sesame oil into a small pan and heat till smoking. Pour into a clean, dry pickling jar. Cover and leave.

Heat one kg sesame oil till smoking. Remove from heat add fenugreek, onion and cumin seeds. Leave to cool.

Put vinegar and jaggery in a pan and stir over moderate heat till jaggery dissolves. Leave to cool.

In a large bowl mix together cooled oil, cooled vinegar and remaining ingredients. Pour into prepared pickling jar. Cover tightly and place in the sun for 10 days. Shake jar from time to time.

This pickle should last one year.

GOBI-SHALGAM KA ACHAAR
Cauliflower and Turnip Pickle

1 kg cauliflower
1 kg turnips
½ kg carrots
3 cups mustard oil
250 gm garlic, peeled and roughly crushed
250 gm ginger, peeled and roughly crushed
½ cup salt
4 tbsp powdered red chilli
750 gm jaggery, crushed
1½ cups malt vinegar
2 tbsp mustard seeds, crushed
2 tbsp garam masala powder

Cut cauliflower into large florets. Peel and cut turnips crosswise into ¼ inch slices. Scrape carrots and cut into 2 by ½ inch pieces. Wash and dry vegetables, spread on a clean cloth and leave for 6-7 hours.

Heat oil in a large pan till smoking. Reduce heat, add garlic and fry till golden. Remove and keep aside.

Add ginger and fry till golden. Add vegetables and reserved garlic and cook, stirring for 10-15 minutes till vegetables are dry. Remove from heat, cover and leave to get completely cold.

Put vinegar and jaggery into a stainless steel pan and stir over low heat till jaggery melts. Remove from heat and keep aside. When completely cold add mustard seeds and garam masala and stir till mixed. Add to cold vegetable mixture with salt and chilli. Mix thoroughly and put into a jar.

Place in the sun for 10-15 days. Stir pickle every day using your hand. (After 2 days taste and add more salt if necessary.)

AAM KA ACHAAR
Mango Pickle

5 kg unripe mangoes
1 kg salt
200 gm turmeric powder
250 gm mustard seeds (rai)
50 gm fenugreek seeds
125 gm aniseed (saunf)
60 gm onion seeds (kalonji)
6 pea-sized pieces asafoetida, ground
3-4 tsp powdered red chilli
500 gm mustard oil

Soak mangoes in cold water for 2 hours.

Cut a small slice off stalk end then cut each mango right through centre (including kernel) into half, then each piece into half again.

Thoroughly wash and dry pieces of mango, rub with salt and turmeric and place in the sun for one day.

Heat mustard oil till smoking. Cool.

Grind mustard seeds finely. Roast fenugreek seeds and pound coarsely. Mix into mangoes along with aniseed, onion seeds, asafoetida and red chilli. Mix well and layer mangoes in a clean pickling jar, pressing down each layer. Pour in mustard oil.

Tie a clean piece of muslin around lid of jar and cover pickle tightly.

Place the jar of pickle in the sun for 10-15 days.

This pickle should last for one year.

HING KI LAUNJI
Mango Pickle with Asafoetida

1 kg unripe mangoes
½ cup salt
2 tsp powdered red chilli
¼ tsp asafoetida

Wash and peel mangoes. Cut lengthwise into ½ inch thick slices. Place in a glass or stainless steel bowl, rub with salt and leave for 6-7 hours. Mix in chilli and asafoetida, put into a covered jar and place in the sun for 4-5 days.

This pickle will stay for about a month.

MEETHI LAUNJI
Sweet Mango Pickle

1 kg unripe mangoes
6 tbsp salt
1 tsp fenugreek seeds (methi dana)
500 gm sugar
1 tsp aniseed (saunf)
1 tsp garam masala
1 tsp powdered red chilli

Wash and peel mangoes. Cut lengthwise into ½ inch thick slices. Place in a glass or stainless steel bowl, rub with salt and leave for 6-7 hours. Soak fenugreek seeds in ½ cup water for 6-7 hours.

Drain liquid from mangoes into a pan and mix in sugar. Stir over medium heat to dissolve sugar. Cook for 2-3 minutes. Add mangoes, fenugreek and remaining spices. Cook for 10-15 minutes till mangoes are translucent. (Shake pan occasionally while cooking.)

Cool and bottle.

This pickle should last for 1-2 months.

HARI MIRCH KA ACHAAR
Green Chilli Pickle

250 gm whole green chillies, with stalks
100 gm tamarind
2-3 tbsp salt
2 tbsp cooking oil
2 tsp aniseed (saunf), roughly crushed
1 tsp fenugreek seeds (methi dana) roughly crushed
100 gm (¾ cup) jaggery (gur) powdered
¼ cup malt vinegar

Wash and dry chillies.

Soak tamarind in one cup hot water for 20 minutes.

Sieve tamarind pulp and keep aside. Discard seeds and fibre. Make lengthwise slits in chillies and sprinkle a little salt inside each. Heat oil in a kadhai or frying pan and fry chillies for 5-7 minutes till they turn white. Reduce heat and add remaining ingredients. Cook, stirring occasionally for 5-10 minutes more till most of the liquid dries and masala clings to chillies. Cool and bottle.

This pickle can be served immediately and keeps for one month.

GAAJAR KA ACHAAR
Carrot Pickle

2 cups thinly sliced carrots
2 tbsp mustard oil
1 tsp mustard seeds (rai)
Pinch asafoetida
1 tsp powdered red chilli
¼ tsp turmeric powder
¼ tsp fenugreek seeds
½ tsp split mustard seeds (rai ki dal)
1 tsp salt
10 cloves garlic, finely sliced
½ cup lime juice

Heat oil and add mustard seed, asafoetida, chilli and turmeric. Fry for one minute and keep aside.

Roast fenugreek seeds and grind with split mustard seeds. Mix into carrots along with salt, garlic and lime juice. Stir in oil mixture.

Put pickle in a jar and keep for 3-4 days before serving.

This pickle should last for one year.

PANI KE BARÉ
Pickled Black Gram Fritters

These pickled baras are traditionally made at Holi.

Fritters:
>250 gm (1¼ cups) husked black beans (dhuli urad ki dal)
>1 inch piece ginger
>2-3 green chillies
>¼ tsp asafoetida
>½ tsp bicarbonate of soda (meetha soda)

>250 gm ghee for frying

Pickling water:
>2 litres water
>1 tbsp salt
>1 level tbsp powdered red chilli
>1½ level tbsp mustard seeds (rai), coarsely crushed

Fritters: Soak black beans in cold water for 8-10 hours.

Drain thoroughly, then grind finely along with ginger, green chillies and asafoetida. Stir in bicarbonate of soda and beat till fluffy. Keep aside.

Heat ghee in a kadhai or wok.

Using wet hands form gram paste into circular fritters on your palm and carefully lower into hot ghee one at a time. Fry, turning once till golden on both sides. Remove from oil and keep aside.

Pickling water: Mix together all ingredients for pickling water and put into a jar. Put in cooled fritters. Cover jar and place in the sun for 3-4 days. These baras keep for one week after they are ready.

Beverages

B efore the advent of bottled drinks, thirst-quenchers were made at home to help one get through the long hot summers.

Even today a freshly made glass of lemonade (neebu pani) is more cooling than any aerated drink.

SHARBAT-E-GULAB
Rose Cordial

Serves: 6-8

A recipe from the *Pukht-o-Paaz*.

750 gm red 'desi' roses
2 litres water
3 kg sugar
250 ml rose water
1½ litres milk, boiled and cooled

Break off rose petals and wash thoroughly. Put into a pan with water and cook on slow fire till liquid has reduced to half.

Strain and add sugar. Return to heat and stir to dissolve sugar. Cook till syrup comes to the boil. Cool and add rose water.

Stir in milk and serve chilled.

AAM KA PANNA
Raw Mango Drink

Serves: 6-8

2 unripe mangoes
½-1 tsp salt
2 tsp sugar
½ tsp roasted, ground cumin seed
Pinch black salt (Kala namak)
Pinch powdered red chillies

Cook mangoes in boiling water for 10-15 minutes till tender. Peel.
Scrape off mango flesh. Mash and stir in remaining ingredients.
To serve, dilute with water and adjust seasoning to taste.

IMLI KA PANNA
Tamarind Drink

Serves: 6-8

150 gm tamarind
½ cup sugar
2 tsp salt
1½ tsp roasted, ground cumin seeds
½ tsp black salt (kala namak)
Pinch powdered red chilli

Soak tamarind in 2 cups hot water for 30 minutes. Sieve pulp and
discard seeds and fibre. Add remaining ingredients and stir to
dissolve sugar. Add 2 cups water, and adjust seasoning to taste.
Chill and serve.

Beverages

ZEERE KA PANI
Spiced Cumin Drink

Serves: 6-8

A recipe from Mrs Sita Nanda.

250 gm tamarind
3 bunches mint
2 heaped tbsp roasted cumin seeds
2 heaped tsp black salt (kala namak)
300-350 gm (1½-1¾ cups) sugar
1 tsp salt
2 tsp powdered red chilli

Soak tamarind in 750 ml cold water for 2 hours. Remove seeds and discard. Put pulp back into soaking water. Keep aside.

Grind mint with cumin and black salt.

Add sugar to tamarind pulp and heat to dissolve. Strain into mint mixture. Add salt and red chilli and strain again through muslin. Add one litre or a little more water.

Chill and serve.

KACHRI KA PANI
A Monsoon Drink

Serves: 4-5

This drink is to be had during the monsoon season.

It is said that the digestive system becomes sluggish during the monsoon—this drink supposedly perks it up!

500 ml water
2 tsp powdered aniseed (saunf)
1 tsp salt
1 tsp black salt
½ tsp powdered red chilli
Pinch asafoetida
2 tsp powdered dried green mango (amchur)
1 tsp ground fresh ginger
Juice of 1 lime
1 tbsp chopped mint leaves
3-4 fresh kachri

Combine all ingredients except kachri.

Peel kachri and remove seeds. Cut into ½ inch pieces and put into the water.

Serve chilled.

Glossary

Almond	:	Badam
Aniseed	:	Saunf
Asafoetida	:	Hing
Aubergine	:	Baigan
Baking soda	:	Meetha soda
Banana, cooking	:	Kaccha kela
Bay leaves	:	Tejpatta
Bengal gram	:	Chane ki dal
Betelnut	:	Supari
Betel leaf	:	Paan
Bitter gourd	:	Karela
Black cardamom	:	Bari elaichi
Black beans, husked	:	Dhuli urad ki dal
Black peppercorns	:	Sabut kali mirch
Black salt	:	Kala namak
Brain	:	Bheja
Bread	:	Double roti
Butter	:	Makhan
Butter, clarified	:	Ghee
Cardamom	:	Chhoti elaichi
Carrot	:	Gaajar
Cauliflower	:	Phool gobi
Cinnamon	:	Dalchini
Chicken	:	Murgh

Chickpea	:	Sufaid chana
Chironji	:	Chironji/Charoli
Cloves	:	Laung
Cluster beans	:	Gwar ki phalli
Coconut	:	Nariyal
Coconut, dried	:	Copra
Colocasia	:	Arvi
Coriander, fresh	:	Hara dhania
Coriander seeds	:	Sabut dhania
Coriander seeds, husked	:	Dhania dana
Cream	:	Cream
Cream of tartar	:	Samundar jhaag
Cucumber	:	Kheera
Cucumber seeds	:	Kheere ke beej
Cumin seeds	:	Zeera
Curd	:	Dahi
Dates	:	Khajoor
Dates, dried	:	Chhuara
Dill	:	Sua bhaji
Egg	:	Anda
Elephant foot yam	:	Zimikand
Fenugreek leaves	:	Methi
Fenugreek seeds	:	Methi dana
Fig	:	Anjeer
Fish	:	Machchi
Flour	:	Maida
Garlic	:	Lehsun
Ginger, dried	:	Sonth
Ginger, fresh	:	Adrak
Gram, green	:	Boont
Gram, parched	:	Bhune chane

Gram flour	:	Besan
Green chillies	:	Hari mirch
Green beans, split	:	Chhilke ki mung ki dal
Green beans, husked	:	Dhuli mung ki dal
Green peas	:	Matar
Head	:	Siri
Jackfruit	:	Kathal
Jaggery	:	Gur
Kidney	:	Gurda
Lentil	:	Dal
Lime	:	Neebu
Liver	:	Kaleji
Lotus seed	:	Makhane
Mace	:	Javitri
Mango	:	Aam
Mango, unripe	:	Ambia/Kairi
Mango, green dried	:	Sabut amchur
Mango, green dried powder	:	Pisa amchur
Marrow	:	Ghia/Lauki
Marsh melon seeds	:	Kharbooze ke beej
Millet	:	Bajra
Milk	:	Doodh
Milk, condensed unsweetened	:	Khoya
Mint	:	Pudina
Mince	:	Keema
Mustard oil	:	Sarson ka tel
Mustard seeds	:	Rai
Mustard seeds, split	:	Rai ki dal
Mustard seeds, yellow	:	Peeli sarson

Mutton	:	Gosht
Nutmeg	:	Jaiphal
Okra	:	Bhindi
Onion	:	Pyaz
Onion seeds	:	Kalaunji
Orange	:	Santra
Papaya, raw	:	Kaccha papeeta
Peas	:	Matar
Pepper (black)	:	Kali mirch
Pickle	:	Achaar
Pigeon peas	:	Arhar ki dal (Toover)
Pistachio nut	:	Pista
Poppy seed	:	Khas-khas
Potato	:	Alu
Pumpkin	:	Kaddu
Pumpkin seeds	:	Kaddu ke beej
Red chillies, whole	:	Sabut lal mirch
Red chillies, powdered	:	Pisi hui lal mirch
Rice	:	Chawal
Rock salt	:	Lahori namak
Rose	:	Gulab ka phool
Rose water	:	Gulabjal
Saffron	:	Zafran/Kesar
Salt	:	Namak
Screwpine flower essence	:	Kewra
Semolina	:	Sooji/Rava
Sesame oil	:	Til ka tel
Sesame seeds	:	Sufaid til
Silver leaf	:	Chandi ki varak
Squash (round)	:	Tinda
Spinach	:	Palak

Sugar	:	Cheeni
Sugar candy	:	Misri
Sugar khandsari	:	Boora
Sultana	:	Kishmish
Tamarind	:	Imli
Thyme	:	Ajwain
Tomato	:	Tamatar
Top of milk	:	Malai/Balai
Trotters	:	Paye
Turmeric	:	Haldi
Turnip	:	Shalgam
Vermicelli	:	Sevian
Vinegar	:	Sirka
Watermelon seeds	:	Tarbooz ke beej
Wax gourd	:	Parval
Wheat	:	Gehun
Wheat porridge	:	Gehun ka dalia
Wholewheat flour	:	Atta
Yoghurt	:	Substitute for dahi

Char Magaz:
A mixture of water melon, marsh melon, cucumber and pumpkin seeds.

Kachri:
A summer fruit which resembles a miniature melon. In its dried form it is used in chutneys and to flavour and tenderise meat.

Kachalu:
A vegetable that looks like a potato and has the texture of colocasia.

Index

FISH

Machchi ke kofte, 86
  (Fish kofta)

Machchi korma, 85
  (Fish curry)

Masala pomfret, 88
  (Whole stuffed pomfret)

Sookhe masale ki machchi, 89
  (Masala fried fish)

LENTILS

Black beans (Urad)
  – Sookhi urad ki dal, 104
  (Dry black beans)

Gram flour (Besan)
  – Kadhi, 109
  (Gram flour curry with
  dumplings)
  – Takke paise, 107
  (Gram flour pennies)

Green beans (Mung)
  – Aalan ka saag, 103
  (Split green beans with
  spinach)
  – Dal ka keema, 101
  (Husked green beans with
  green peas)
  – Dal ki kaleji, 99
  (Green bean cubes in gravy)
  – Dal ki pakori, 97
  (Green bean fritters in gravy)

  – Mung dal aur palak, 105
  (Green beans with spinach)

Mangori
  – Sookhi mangori, 94
  (Dried mangori)
  – Tali mangori, 96
  (Fried mangori)

Pigeon peas (Arhar)
  – Mandhiya, 106
  (Pigeon peas in rice konji)

MASALA/POWDERED SPICES

Chaat ka masala, 241
  (Chaat masala)

Garam masala, 13

MUTTON

Alu ka saalan, 39
  (Mutton with potatoes)

Babu Shahi's kundan kalia, 33
  (White mutton)

Brain
  – Bheja methi, 69
  (Brain with fenugreek)
  – Bhunva bheja, 68
  (Curried brain)

Curries
  – Do piaza - 1, 27
  (Mutton curry with onions)